T0208905

Growing in Grace and the Knowledge of God

GETTING TO KNOW THE GOD OF THE BIBLE

NORMAN WILSON

authorHOUSE®

AuthorHouse™
1663 Liberty Drive
Bloomington, IN 47403
www.authorhouse.com
Phone: 1 (800) 839-8640

Published by AuthorHouse 04/16/2019

ISBN: 978-1-7283-0850-0 (sc)
ISBN: 978-1-7283-0849-4 (e)

Print information available on the last page.

This book is printed on acid-free paper.

CONTENTS

INTRODUCTION

The apostle Peter closes his second epistle with these insightful words, "But grows in grace and knowledge of our Lord and Savior Jesus Christ." This should be the heart's desire of every Christian, and the quest of those who seek the true means of eternal salvation.

God designed every human being with the capacity to know and understand that He is truly God. This knowledge of Himself is revealed through His creation (Romans 1:20), the Bible (John 20:31), His Son (John 14:9), the Holy Spirit (John 16:13), and the conscience (Romans 2:14-15). The Holy Spirit may use any or all of these to awaken the human spirit to understand that God is real, and the only means of attaining eternal life. Biblical truths are verified by a person's spirit and not necessarily by his intellect.

The purpose of this entire book is to provide guideposts that will help those earnestly seeking the truth about God. I trust it will also aid fellow Christians in understanding their God and His unconditional love for them. My goal is to provide food for spiritual thought and not a thesis for intellectual argument.

The current world system is saturated with innumerable religious organizations, groups, sects, cults, and occults. Most of these offer their followers a means of eternal security. Christianity sets itself a part from all these by declaring that the Christian bible contains the only true revelations about God. They assert the bible gives instructions on how to have a relationship with God, and directions for attaining eternal salvation. How can Christianity state with such assurance that its way is the only way to attain this relationship with God and have eternal life?

This book is written with the expressed purpose of presenting evidences relating to Christian doctrines; the only means of experiencing a relationship with the one true God and obtaining eternal life. I have also tried to offer some helps to challenge the Christian to examine some of the controversial doctrines being taught. This book is only a gateway to discovering biblical truths about God. It is offered as an appetizer not the full meal to those who truly wish to taste and see that the Lord is good.

I do not pretend by writing this book to have attained the high ground of biblical maturity. I believe this should be the progressive goal of every earnest Christian. Instead I have attempted to share revelations to help guide the individual in the process of Christian growth.

The reader is encouraged to seek revelation from the Holy Spirit as he studies the scriptures presented in this book. My desire is for this study to whet the reader's appetite to explore more of this inexhaustible topic. The study of God is in some ways similar to panning gold, every nugget discovered is valuable. There are many things about God that will only be discovered by the diligent search of the scriptures. Some aspects of the gospel are repeated in different formats throughout this book to reinforce the reception of these truths.

CHAPTER ONE

The beginning, God's purpose.

Any study that declares Christianity is the only way of attaining eternal life must present sufficient evidence to support this claim. This evidence must provide a biblical basis to support why salvation can only be secured by believing the bible version of God's plan for mankind. The Bible reveals the nature of God and declares that He created the entire universe, and has complete control over all His creation. It also records the beginning of mankind and God's relationship to the human race. If these claims are true then the Bible is beyond doubt the single most important book that an individual can read, study, and apply during his time on earth. (For irrefutable evidence of why one should believe the bible the serious searcher should read Evidence That Demands a Verdict by Josh McDowell or Google "Why I believe the bible" and read for themselves the overwhelming proofs of the validity of the bible).

In order for a person to receive and understand truth he must seek truth with an open and inquiring mind and heart. However, he must also be careful to develop safeguards against erroneous interpretations of the scriptures. The words of God as recorded in the bible will resonate with truth in a person's spirit because they are spiritual and contain life (John 6:63, Hebrews 4:12).

The truths of the bible can be validated by: 1 – Examining all the reasons given why one should accept the reliability of the Bible. 2- How what is presented remains consistent throughout the bible, how it harmonizes with other scripture, and if it is believable in the context in which it is given? 3- How it has weathered the scrutiny of critics and remained valid? 4- Determining if it has it worked in the lives of those who teach it, and does it work in the lives of others?

The Christian bible is God's record of His existence, His creation, His purpose, and redemption of mankind. It records His unconditional love for all men, and provides a glimpse of eternity past and future. In eternity past God desired to have a species of beings that were created in His image. That He could include as part of His family and lavish His love upon. The Holy Trinity, God the Father, God the Son, and God the Holy Spirit, in council devised the best means of causing this to happen. (This plan will be discussed in greater depth under the section of "Redeeming Grace").

This story of how God created man in His own image is recorded in the early chapters of the book of Genesis. He created Adam and Eve with a pure heart and soul and gave them the freedom to eat the fruit of every tree in the garden including the Tree of Life. However, He strictly warned them not to eat the fruit of the Tree of the Knowledge of Good and Evil for if they did they would die. The choices were clearly defined; to eat of the Tree of Life was to continue with God in the grace life for eternity. To choose to eat of the Tree of the Knowledge of Good and Evil was to choose death and separation from the source of eternal life. Why Adam and Eve failed to see the dreadful consequences of making the wrong choice will never be known until we are given greater revelation in heaven.

God knew that Adam would eat the fruit of the Tree of the Knowledge of Good and Evil and it would cause him and all mankind to be separated from Him. Therefore, before He created the foundation of the world God devised a plan through which every individual would be offered an invitation to share eternal life with Him. This plan was initiated, established, executed, and concluded through the birth, life, ministry, death on the cross, and resurrection of His Son, the Lord Jesus Christ.

God placed Adam and Eve in the perfect environment of the garden. He provided everything they needed to be His representatives of grace in the world. The garden was to be a base from which the descendants of Adam would populate the earth. They were to demonstrate the image of God throughout all the earth.

The devil corrupted this environment by deceiving Adam and Eve. He led them to believe that if they ate of the fruit of the Tree of the Knowledge of Good and Evil they would be more like God. They evidently believed that eating of the forbidden fruit would improve their likeness of God. Sadly to say this scam of believing there is something we can do to make us more like God is still used by the devil today. Only God can create one in His own image. There is nothing man can do through his own efforts that can improve on what God has done. They may have also planned to eat of the Tree of Life at a later time. However, once they had eaten of the Tree of the Knowledge of Good and Evil they no longer had access to the Tree of Life. From our vantage point we can clearly see the foolishness of the choice they made. But, a cursory examination of worldly religions will reveal that many are still making similar choices. These are just as detrimental to where they will spend eternity.

The God of the Bible is holy and His kingdom is a kingdom of righteousness. A person must also be righteous to have an eternal relationship with Him. However, man in his fallen state can never attain the righteousness required to fellowship with God. God's plan of redemption provides this righteousness as a gift to all who will believe in His Son for salvation.

The core of this plan includes Jesus coming to earth to reveal exactly what God is like, and to present God's plan of redemption to mankind. The plan is very simple, a person must believe what Jesus taught and demonstrated through His life. That He is the Son of God, and the only means of acquiring eternal life (John 14:6). When a person believes this his human spirit is born again eternally, and he is counted as righteous to enjoy an eternal relationship with God.

Because God exists in eternity He is able to comprehend all of eternity in His scope of vision and knowledge. Time was created by God for mankind. Time is a parenthesis on the line of eternity; it has a beginning and an end. It is a capsule that God provides which allows mankind the opportunity to relate to God and decide their destiny. It is a sphere where human beings regardless of color, ethnic background, race, status, or role are meant to live in the harmony of God's love and grace.

God desires Christians to be His representatives by expressing the characteristics of their new nature to those in their sphere of influence in the world. Individuals can do this by showing love, compassion, mercy, kindness, and other godly acts and attitudes to others. Time provides individuals with the opportunity to learn how to live in harmony. Jesus operated within this time capsule to provide the redemption of fallen mankind. When He declared from the cross, "It is finished", He was saying, "Dad We did it! Now it is a done deal for eternity.

The Christian bible instructs us to grow in grace and the knowledge of God (II Peter 3:18). The individual improves his understanding and intimacy with God through his pursuit of biblical and experiential knowledge of God. Those who acquire this knowledge gain a deeper understanding of God and how He manifests the many facets of His grace to mankind. In addition he will assume the responsibility of expressing God's grace to others. The more we understand about the nature and essence of God the more we will trust Him. We will also gain a better understanding of the interpretation and application of many difficult passages of scripture.

God's essence of love compels His actions and relations to all mankind. A failure to understand that the true nature of God is unconditional love has caused many to have a distorted image of God. This has led to a misunderstanding of God's intent toward His creation. As a Christian grows in the knowledge and grace of God he is able to communicate more effectively the true nature of God to the lost, and guide other Christians to embrace these truths.

The gospel is the manifestation of God's grace toward mankind. The biblical word for "gospel" has several meanings, but all of them express the "good news" of what God has done to recover and establish a relationship with mankind. It means to share the good news of God's love to others for the purpose of introducing them to the true God who loves them.

The following chapters are submitted as evidence that the God of the bible is the true God and His plan for the redemption of mankind is the only means for man's salvation

CHAPTER TWO

The source of eternal life

The very core of most religions is their doctrine of how an individual obtains eternal life, the means of overcoming physical death. There are as many doctrines as there are religions that declare how this immortality can be achieved. However, for those who believe the bible is given to us by inspiration from God, eternal life can only be acquired by believing in Jesus Christ as the Son of God. If this is the only way for a person to receive eternal life it would be vital for him to thoroughly examine the basis of this belief.

The inquiring individual will acknowledge that everything that exists from the minute atom to the vastness of the universe has the trade mark of a divine designer. They will also have difficulty believing that such a complex creation just evolved from nothing without some outside source. Christians believe this source to be God. We believe that there is only one true God, and that He exists in the persons of the Father, Son, and Holy Spirit. We believe that it was God who created all things, and therefore He Himself was not created. If God is not created, and there is such a thing as eternal life, then only God is eternal and the only source of eternal life. Our conclusion is that eternal life only exists in the Holy Trinity of the Father, Son, and Holy Spirit. Eternal life is not something that can be attained it can only be received when shared by the Trinity.

Everything that exists whether seen or unseen was created by God and has a span of existence as determined by Him. Therefore, every created thing outside the Godhead can only exist for the length of time its creator designed it to last, and this includes mankind. Regardless of the length of its existence nothing created outside the Trinity has eternal qualities or the ability to give eternal life.

Matthew 24:35 – Heaven and earth will pass away, but My words will by no means pass away.

II Peter 3:10 - But the day of the Lord will come as a thief in the night, in which the heavens will pass away with a great noise, and the elements will melt with fervent heat; both the earth and the works that are in it will be burned up.

Revelation 21:1 – Now I saw a new heaven and a new earth, for the first heaven and the first earth had passed away. Also there was no more sea.

If uncreated God is the only source of eternal life it would be reasonable and biblically sound to conclude that the only way for a person to obtain eternal life is by being placed into the Trinity. This is a feat that is impossible for any created being to accomplish. It can only be attained by God allowing a person to share His life. The Bible reveals that this is exactly what God formulated, executed, and fulfilled through the life and ministry of Jesus Christ, His Son.

When a person believes in Jesus the scriptures say that he is born again. His spirit become one with the Spirit of God. It is a union whereby man's spirit and God's Spirit are indistinguishable. Only after this takes place and man's spirit has its source in God's Spirit does he have eternal life, and able to live the life desired of him as recorded in the bible.

The choice of eternal life was first offered to Adam and Eve. They were given the choice to eat of the Tree of Life and live forever. They were already living souls (Genesis 2:7, Genesis 3:22). They were also free to eat of the Tree of the Knowledge of Good and Evil, but God warned them that if they ate of its fruit they would die. In their original state they were given the opportunity to choose life or death. This is the choice that God still offers all mankind.

Instead of choosing the Tree of Life they were influenced by Satan to choose temporal knowledge which led to death. Adam is the father of all mankind so his choice caused all of his descendants to be born spiritually separated from God, the source of eternal life. This condition remained until the death of Jesus on the cross once again made it possible for those who believe in Him to have eternal life. In essence He became the Tree of life.

The biblical account of the life and ministry of Jesus reveals that He alone as the Son of God was qualified to offer His life as a sacrifice so that all of mankind could be reconciled to God. Jesus, the last Adam, was God's representative to recover all that was lost through the wrong choice of the first Adam. Jesus' sacrifice makes it possible for individuals to choose eternal life offered by God through belief in His Son.

The only biblical means of attaining eternal life is through Jesus Christ, the Son of God, there is no other option. When a person believes that Jesus is the Son of God, and what He taught and demonstrated about God is true a spiritual birth that takes place. That person' spirit is born again and becomes one with the Spirit of Jesus, and he has eternal life.

<u>I Corinthians 15:45-49</u> – And so it is written, "The first man Adam became a living being". The last Adam became a life-giving spirit. (46) However, the spiritual is not first, but the natural, and afterward the spiritual. (47) The first man was of the earth, made of dust; the second Man is the Lord from heaven. (48) As was the man of dust, so also are those who are made of dust; and as is the heavenly Man, so also are those who are heavenly. (49) And as we have borne the image of the man of dust, we shall also bear the image of the heavenly Man.

<u>I Corinthians 15: 44</u> – It is sown a natural body, it is raised a spiritual body. There is a natural body, and there is a spiritual body.

<u>II Corinthian 5:14-15</u> For the love of Christ compels us, because we judge thus: that if <u>One died for all, then all died;</u> (15) and <u>He died for all,</u> that those who live should live no longer for themselves, but for Him who died for them and rose again.

<u>Romans 6:8</u> – Now if we died with Christ, we believe that we shall also live with Him.

The following scriptures are offered as verification to be meditated upon. Portions of certain scriptures are underlined to help the reader easily see their emphasis.

A. <u>God is the only true God:</u>

- <u>Isaiah 46:9</u> – Remember the former things of old, for I am God, and <u>there is no other</u>; I am God, and there is none like Me.

- Mark 12:29 – Jesus answered him, "The first of all the commandments is; Hear, O Israel, the Lord our God, the Lord is one.
- Galatians 3:20 – Now a mediator does not meditate for one only, but God is one.
- Ephesians 4:6 One God and Father of all, who is above all, and through all, and in you all.

B. Trinity: God the Father, God the Son, and God the Holy Spirit as one.

- Matthew 3:16-17 – When He had been baptized, Jesus came up immediately from the water; and behold, the heavens were opened to Him, and He saw the Spirit of God descending like a dove and alighting upon Him. (17) And suddenly a voice came from heaven saying, "This is My beloved Son, in whom I am well pleased. (Father)
- Matthew 28:19 – Go therefore and make disciples of all the nations, baptizing them in the name of the Father and of the Son and of the Holy Spirit.
- John 14:16-17 – And I will pray the Father, and He will give you another Helper, that He may abide with you forever – (17) the Spirit of truth, whom the world cannot receive because it neither sees Him nor knows him; but you know Him, for He dwells with you and will be in you.
- II Corinthians 13:14 – The grace of the Lord Jesus Christ, and the love of God, and the communion of the Holy Spirit be with you all. Amen.

C. Eternal life exists in God alone.

- John 17:3 – And this is eternal life, that they may know You, the only true God, and Jesus Christ whom You have sent.
- John 1:4 – In Him was life, and the life was the light of men.

- John 10:27-30 – My sheep hear My voice, and I know them, and they follow Me. (28) And I give them eternal life, and they shall never perish; neither shall anyone snatch them out of My hand. (29) My father, who has given them to Me, is greater than all; and no one is able to snatch them out of My Father's hand. (30) I and My Father are one.
- John 3:14-16 – And as Moses lifted up the serpent in the wilderness, even so must the Son of Man be lifted up, (15) that whoever believes in Him should not perish but have eternal life. (16) For God so loved the world that He gave His only begotten Son, that whoever believe in Him should not perish but have everlasting life.
- I John 5:11-13 – And this is the testimony; that God has given us eternal life, and this life is in His Son. (12) He who has the Son has life; he who does not have the Son of God does not have life. (13) These things I have written to you who believe in the name of the Son of God, that you may know that you have eternal life, and that you may continue to believe in the name of the Son of God.
- Romans 6:23 – for the wages of sin is death, but the gift of God is eternal life in Christ Jesus our Lord.

D. The new birth seals us in Christ and secures us eternally.

- Ephesians 1:13-14 – In Him you also trusted, after you heard the word of truth, the gospel of your salvation; in whom also, having believed, you were sealed with the Holy spirit of promise, (14) who is the guarantee of our inheritance until the redemption of the purchased possession, to the praise of His glory.
- Romans 10:9-10 – That if you confess with your mouth the Lord Jesus and believe in your heart that God has raised Him from the dead, you will be saved. (10) for with the heart one believes unto righteousness, and with the mouth confession is made unto salvation.

- I Corinthians 12:13 – For by one Spirit we were all baptized into one body – whether Jews or Greeks, whether slaves or free – and have all been made to drink into one Spirit.
- Romans 6:3-4 – Or do you not know that as many of us as were baptized into Christ Jesus were baptized into His death? (4) Therefore we were buried with Him through baptism into death, that just as Christ was raised from the dead by the glory of the father, even so we also should walk in newness of life.
- Galatians 3:26-28 – For you are all sons of God through faith in Christ Jesus. (27) For as many of you as were baptized into Christ have put on Christ. (28) There is neither Jew nor Greek, there is neither slave nor free, there is neither male nor female; for you are all one in Christ Jesus.
- I Corinthians 15: 44-45 – It is sown a natural body, it is raised a spiritual body. There is a natural body, and there is a spiritual body. (45) And so it is written, "The first man Adam became a living being." The last Adam became a life-giving spirit.

There is much debate among theologians and laymen alike about the immortality of the human spirit; however, one truth that should be considered is the fact that if a person must believe in Jesus for his spirit to be born again and have eternal life, then that person's spirit must not have possessed eternal qualities prior.

CHAPTER THREE

Jesus Christ, God's only means of Eternal Life.

Most religions offer their followers a belief system that assures them of eternity in a place of bliss and contentment. A person does not have to be an astute student of religious beliefs to understand that all these claims can not be true, and if not, which is true? The Christian doctrine declares Jesus to be the Son of God, and belief in Him as the only means of forgiveness of sin and eternal life.

A person's theology determines where he will spend eternity. Therefore, it is certainly worth his while to examine the evidence that Jesus alone is the only means of obtaining eternal life. The validation of spiritual truth is a function of the spirit of man and may or may not be confirmed by the mind or intellect of a person. The Holy Spirit gives biblical revelation to a person through the human spirit (John 26:13).

The following scriptures and comments regarding the Christian doctrine of salvation are offered for those earnestly seeking truth.

The bible states a person must be born again to have eternal life and go to heaven.

> John 3:1-6 – There was a man of the Pharisees named Nicodemus, a ruler of the Jews. (2) This man came to Jesus by night and said to Him, "Rabbi, we know that You are a teacher come from God; for no one can do these signs that You do unless God is with him. (3) Jesus answered and said to him, "Most assuredly, I say to you,

> unless one is born again, he cannot see the kingdom of God. (4) Nicodemus said to Him, "How can a man be born when he is old? Can he enter a second time into his mother's womb and be born? (5) Jesus answered, "Most assuredly, I say to you, "unless one is born of water and the Spirit, he cannot enter the kingdom of God. (6) That which is born of the flesh is flesh, and that which is born of the Spirit is spirit.

Jesus declares that one must be born of the Holy Spirit to enter the spiritual kingdom of God. Nicodemus responds with "How can a man be born again"? This very important question has puzzles the mind of many seekers through the centuries. However, Jesus explains that to be born again means one must experience a spiritual birth after he is born physically. A person is born physically after the water sac in the womb of the mother is broken. The spiritual birth takes place when an individual believes in Jesus as the Son of God. The Holy Spirit gives their spirit new life and places them into the Spirit of Jesus.

I Corinthians 12:13 – For by one Spirit we were all baptized into one body – whether Jews or Greeks, whether slaves or free – and have all been made to drink into one Spirit.

Galatians 2:20 – I have been crucified with Christ; it is no longer I who live, but Christ lives in me; and the life which I now live in the flesh I live by faith in the Son of God, who loved me and gave Himself for me.

I Corinthians 15:50 –Now this I say, brethren, that flesh and blood cannot inherit the kingdom of God; nor does corruption inherit incorruption.

1. Why a person must be born again.

When God placed Adam in the garden He warned him that he would die if he ate of the fruit of the Tree of the Knowledge of Good and Evil (Genesis 2:17). Theologians have agreed that this was a spiritual death since Adam continued to live for more than nine hundred years. Death is a separation; physical death occurs when a person's spirit leaves their body

(James 2:26), spiritual death is the separation of the human spirit from God, the source of life (Ephesians 4:18).

Adam sinned by eating fruit from the Tree of the Knowledge of Good and Evil which caused him to die spiritually, be separated from God. This death was passed down to his children and through them to all mankind. Therefore, every human being is born spiritually separated from God (Romans 5:12). Only God can cause the human spirit to be born again with eternal life. He does this at the moment a person puts their trust in Jesus Christ, His Son. Jesus was explaining to Nicodemus that a person's spirit must be born from above by the Holy Spirit to enter the Kingdom of God (John 3:1-8).

> Genesis 2:17 – But of the tree of the knowledge of good and evil you shall not eat, for in the day that you eat of it you shall surely die. (spiritually)
>
> Romans 5:12 –Therefore, just as through one man sin entered the world, and death through sin, and thus death spread to all men, because all sinned.(Spiritual death)
>
> James 2:26 – For as the body without the spirit is dead, so faith without works is dead also. (Physical death)
>
> Ephesians 4:18 – having their understanding darkened, being alienated from the life of God, because of the ignorance that is in them, because of the blindness of their heart.
>
> John 5:24 – Most assuredly, I say to you, he who hears My word and believes in Him who sent Me has everlasting life, and shall not come into judgment, but has passed from death into life.
>
> Ephesians 2:1 – And you He made alive, who were dead in trespasses and sins.
>
> Colossians 2:13 – And you, being dead in your trespasses and the uncircumcision of your flesh, He has made alive together with Him, having forgiven you all trespasses.

Jesus was not a descendant of Adam. He was conceived by the Holy Spirit through the Virgin Mary. Since He was not conceived by an earthly father He did not inherit the sin nature handed down from Adam. It is crucial to understand that if Jesus had been born of an earthly father His spirit would have been separated from God like all mankind. He would not have been qualified to die for the sins of others because He would also have been born a sinner.

I Peter 1:18-19 –knowing that you were not redeemed with corruptible things, like silver or gold, from your aimless conduct received by tradition from your fathers, (19) but with the precious blood of Christ, as of a lamb without blemish and without spot.

2. Eternal life is given to us at our new birth as a gift of God's grace.

> Ephesians 2:8-9 - For by grace you have been saved through faith, and that not of yourselves; it is the gift of God, (9) Not of works, lest anyone should boast.
>
> Romans 6:23 – For the wages of sin is death, but the gift of God is eternal life in Christ Jesus our Lord.
>
> Colossians 2:13 – And you, being dead in your trespasses and the uncircumcision of your flesh, He has made alive together with Him, having forgiven you all trespasses.
>
> John 1:13 – who were born, not of blood, nor of the will of the flesh, nor of the will of man, but of God.

3. Why God offer salvation through grace as a free gift.

God's plan for the redemption of mankind is called the "gospel". Although it is free to mankind it cost the Son of God the sacrifice of His life. God's plan before the foundation of the world was to create a species of humans that He could have a relationship with and love. This plan included the reconciliation of mankind through the life, death, and resurrection of His Son. When Jesus died on the cross as the spotless Lamb of God, He died in the place of every sinner so we could be reconciled to God, and have all our sins forgiven. Because Jesus died for all sins God offers the gift of eternal life to all who will trust Him for their redemption.

Galatians 1:4 – Who gave Himself for our sins, that He might deliver us from this present evil age, according to the will of our God and Father.

Romans 5:10 – For if when we were enemies we were reconciled to God trough the death of His Son, much more, having been reconciled, we shall be saved by His life.

II Corinthians 5:18-19 – Now all things are of God, who has reconciled us to Himself through Jesus Christ, and has given to us the ministry of reconciliation. (19) that is, that God was in Christ reconciling the world to Himself, not imputing their trespass to them, and has committed to us the word of reconciliation.

Jesus dealt with the sin problem when He died in our place, freeing us to have power over sin. God has given us the gift of righteousness which empowers us to live godly.

Romans 5:17 – For if by the one man's offense death reigned through the one, much more those who receive abundance of grace and of the gift of righteousness will reign in life through the One, Jesus Christ.

II Corinthians 5:21 – for He made Him who knew no sin to be sin for us, that we might become the righteousness of God in Him.

Romans 6:14 – For sin shall not have dominion over you, for you are not under law but under grace.

4. Theologians acknowledge that Jesus' death on the cross included the forgiveness of all sins, past – present – future.

- I Peter 2:24 – Who Himself bore our sins in His own body on the tree, that we, having died to sins, might live for righteousness – by whose stripes you were healed.
- Colossians 2:13-14 – And you, being dead in your trespasses and the uncircumcision of your flesh, He has made alive together with Him, having forgiven you all trespasses. (14) having wiped out the hand-writing of requirements that was against us, which was contrary to us. And He has taken it out of the way, having nailed it to the cross.
- I John 2:2 – And He Himself is the propitiation for our sins, and not for ours only but also for the whole world.
- Hebrews 10: 12,14,17 – But this Man, after He had offered one sacrifice for sins forever sat down at the right hand of God, (14) For by one offering He has perfected forever those who are being sanctified. (17) Then He adds, "Their sins and their lawless deeds I will remember no more.
- John 1:29 – The next day John saw Jesus coming toward him, and said, "Behold! The Lamb of God who takes away the sins of the world!
- Romans 4: 7-8 – Blessed are those whose lawless deeds are forgiven and whose sins are covered. (8) Blessed is the man to whom the Lord shall not impute sin.
- Hebrews 10: 17-18 – then He adds, "Their sins and their lawless deeds I will remember no more. (18) Now where there is remission of these, there is no longer an offering for sin.

Sin may be defined as any thought, attitude, or action that is in violation of the righteous principles governing the Kingdom of God, as outlined in the Scriptures. Those that obey these biblical principles reap the benefits outlined in these rules of conduct and life. But to break them inherently causes some measure of adverse effects in the lives of those who violate them. This is the consequences of individual sins. Often the consequences are just the opposite of the benefits of following the righteous principles of the Kingdom of God.

5. When a person expresses faith in Jesus as the Son of God his spirit is born again by the Holy Spirit.

> Romans 10:9-10 – That if you confess with your mouth the Lord Jesus and believe in your heart that God has raised Him from the dead, you will be saved. (10) For with the heart one believes unto righteousness, and with the mouth confession is made unto salvation.
>
> John 3:16 –For God so loved the world that He gave His only begotten Son, that whoever believes in Him should not perish but have everlasting life.
>
> John 5:24 – Most assuredly, I say to you, he who hears My word and believes in Him who sent Me has everlasting life, and shall not come into judgment, but has pass from death into life.
>
> I Peter 1:23 – Having been born again, not of corruptible seed but incorruptible, through the word of God which lives and abides forever.
>
> John 1:1 – In the beginning was the Word, and the Word was with God, and the Word was God.

6. A person' spirit becomes eternal when the Holy Spirit places him into Jesus.

> I Corinthians 12:13 – For by one Spirit we were all baptized into one body – whether Jews or Greeks, whether slaves or free – and have all been made to drink into one Spirit.
>
> Romans 6:3-6,8 – Or do you not know that as many of us as were baptized into Christ Jesus were baptized into His death.(4) Therefore we were buried with Him through baptism into death, that just as Christ was raised from the dead by the glory of the Father, even so we also should

walk in newness of life. (5) For if we have been united together in the likeness of His death, certainly we also shall be in the likeness of His resurrection,(6) Knowing this, that our old man was crucified with Him, that the body of sin might be done away with, that we should no longer be slaves of sin, (8) Now if we died with Christ, we believe that we shall also live with Him.

I John 5:11-12 – And this is the testimony: that God has given us eternal life, and this life is in His Son. (12) He who has the Son has life; he who does not have the Son of God does not have life.

The moment we believe in Jesus we are born again spiritually. Our spirit becomes one with Him and we share His eternal life, crucifixion and resurrection.

CHAPTER FOUR

The Kingdom of God

Understanding the aspects of the Kingdom of God is vital to the health, prosperity, fruitfulness, happiness, power and general wellbeing of the Christian. A priority of Jesus' ministry was preaching and demonstrating the principles of His Kingdom. Through past decades there has been a shifting from a focus on the Kingdom to many other doctrinal focuses, such as the Church, the Bible, evangelism, and discipleship. The Kingdom includes all of these and they are valuable assets of the Kingdom. However, when they become the main focus to the exclusion of the magnificent intent of the Kingdom, they present only a limited understanding of the gospel of the Kingdom. Jesus never said, seek you first the Church, He never said seek you first the Bible or evangelism, He said, "Seek you first the Kingdom of God".

The Church is an essential entity within the Kingdom. The purpose of the Church is to train and educate Christians in the ways and concepts of the Kingdom. The focus of evangelism is the salvation of the lost. This is a worthy cause, but evangelism within itself does not demonstrate many other meaningful aspects of the Kingdom of God. The Kingdom of God can not be advanced without evangelizing people. The same is true of the Church. Whenever the Kingdom advances the church also grows. In the book of Acts we see the advancement of the Kingdom and the growth of the Church as a byproduct. The bible is essential to understanding the Kingdom. However, bible knowledge without living application of its teachings fails to demonstrate Kingdom characteristics to the lost world.

1. The Essence of the Kingdom of God.

In eternity past God created a spiritual realm that He calls Heaven. This realm is inhabited by spiritual beings also created by God. He reigns sovereign as King over all He has created. All beings in this kingdom are submitted to His divine will. They exist for His pleasure and service. This realm of His rule, authority, and influence is called the Kingdom of Heaven. God extended His Kingdom by creating the earth and mankind to populate it. His reign over Heaven and earth is called the Kingdom of God. The essence of this Kingdom is the very nature of God.

Different types of perfumes are created by mixing ingredients that produce individual fragrances. These aromas are not the essence but are the results produced by the mixture, which is the essence. The same is true of the Kingdom. The functions and actions of the Kingdom such as love, compassion, kindness, healing, deliverance, etc., are only the manifestations of the essence of the Kingdom, which is the nature of God.

The Kingdom may be likened to leaven or yeast which is placed in dough to change the nature of the dough. The Holy Spirit within individuals motivates them to conform to the image of Christ. This enables them to release the essence of His Kingdom. Just as a grain of corn placed into the ground will die and come back alive in a new form, the Christian placed into Christ dies, and is born again as a new creation with a divine nature capable of expressing the nature of the Kingdom.

God spoke the universe and all its components into being. Divine forensics will show that all creation bears His trademark. The laws of His creation were designed to remain constant and dependable through the ages. Within the physical universe the laws governing matter, gravity, elements, gaseous components, molecular makeup, atom construction, etc., are constants. Man is able to fly to the moon, land and return to earth based upon mathematical formulas, gravity, combustion of fuels, communications through airwaves, and many other constants. The laws of the Kingdom of God also remain constant and can be relied upon to always produce the results they promise.

God also created Adam and Eve and place them in the perfect garden on earth. They were to populate the earth with their descendants who would demonstrate the essence of His kingdom throughout the earth. God desired that Adam's descendants express His nature to future generations.

God created man in His own image to rule over this physical portion of His kingdom and to express the essence of His Kingdom.

> *"Then God said, "Let Us make man in Our image, according to Our likeness, let them have dominion over the fish of the sea, over the birds of the air, and over the cattle, over all the earth and over every creeping thing that creeps on the earth." Genesis 1:26*
>
> *Then God blessed them, and God said to them, "Be fruitful and multiply; fill the earth and subdue it; have dominion over the fish of the sea, over the birds of the air, and over every living thing that moves on the earth.*
>
> *Genesis 1:28*

God designed Adam with a physical body where His Spirit could reside and influence his actions. He also gave him a soul, and spirit through which He could manifest the essence of His nature. Adam's entire being was designed to function in harmony with all the attributes of God's Kingdom. God breathed into him, and Adam became a living, active being. Adam's role was to express the heart of God and extend His Kingdom in the physical world as the model for all future humans. To accomplish this required Adam to eat of the Tree of Life and receive God's eternal Spirit. When Adam instead disobeyed God by eating the fruit of the Tree of the Knowledge of Good and Evil, his spirit was separated from God. He was no longer capable of demonstrating the nature of God or the guiding principles of the Kingdom. He forfeited eternal life and no longer qualified to be God's representative for His earthly Kingdom.

Adam's descendants are still designed by God to house His Spirit. But, now their thoughts, actions, and attitudes are controlled by a lower sinful nature as a result of Adam's fall. Without the Spirit of God they are incapable of expressing what God and His Kingdom are like. This was the state of all mankind until the coming of Jesus Christ.

God has never deviated from His desire to have fellowship with human beings. Through the death of His Son on the cross He has provided a way for every individual to have eternal life, and qualify to represent Him on the earth. Jesus' ministry was to restore mankind to a position that enables them to receive spiritual life from the God

Man in his fallen condition could not demonstrate the Kingdom of God on earth. This could not be fully accomplished until Jesus came. Jesus, as King, was the only one qualified to demonstrate the aspects of His Kingdom. His life expressed the nature of the Father, and the divine principles of the Kingdom. He provided Christians with an example of how to exercise the attributes of the Kingdom. Jesus was the personification of the Kingdom because His entire being body, soul, and spirit expressed the Father's nature.

The born again divine nature of man is totally compatible with the fundamental nature of the Kingdom. He is capable of receiving and assimilating the life truths of the Kingdom. These truths, statutes, principles, concepts, and precepts are necessary for the wellbeing of the individual. To violate them causes serious problems in the person's spiritual, physical, and emotional condition. These attributes provide holistic wellbeing at every level of human experience and relationships. Most if not all of man's problems and sicknesses can be attributed to the violation of these principles.

Computers have hard drives capable of storing many gigabytes of programs for various activities. The computer hard drive can only express its internal programs through a monitor. The monitor does not house or activate the programs. It can only reflect what the hard drive dictates. Computers only perform the functions of the programs stored within them. In a similar manner, we can only express externally what is internalized within our spirit

I. Life Principles of the Kingdom

Christians are promised that everything they need to grow in grace and live godly lives has been made available to them. Jesus states that seeking the Kingdom of God and His righteousness is the means of acquiring these things. Seeking the Kingdom of God is discovering and applying the biblical principles as revealed by the Holy Spirit. Christians have been given the ability to understand and apply these spiritual precepts in their lives. The functions and attributes of the Kingdom relate to every aspect of our lives. Individual's lives are enriched when they apply these principles as guidelines in their daily activities.

- II Peter 1:3 – as His divine power has given to us all things that pertain to life and godliness, through the knowledge of Him who called us by glory and virtue.
- Matthew 6:33 – But seek first the kingdom of God and His righteousness, and all these things shall be added to you.
- Matthew 13:11 – He answered and said to them, "Because it has been given to you to know the mysteries of the kingdom of heaven, but to them it has not been given

God gives men the wisdom to understand the function and structure of the way He designed matter and elements of the physical world. Men use this knowledge to develop substance, theories, and procedures that benefit society. Men discover a portion of something God has created such as the atom or the spectrum of light. They develop theories and write books containing their understandings of these subjects. Years later, God reveals to others that these were just partial findings, and gives other benefits for their use.

Both history and science record these discoveries. Electricity, sound waves, radio waves etc. were all part of the original creation. However, Adam did not have electric lights and Abraham did not have a smart phone. The current use of digital technology is a prime example of man advancing his knowledge about something God created in the beginning.

We can also say this is true of the principles of God's Kingdom. God constantly gives greater revelation of the truths and concepts of His Kingdom to interested individuals. Some of the basic principles of the Kingdom are: faith, purity, holiness, righteousness, honesty, love, peace and joy. There are spiritual, emotional, and physical benefits for exercising these principles in a person's life. Men write books on how the application of these attributes have benefited their lives. Others read the books to gain insight on how they may also apply them in their lives. Men will continue to write books as God gives progressive revelation about the principle of His Kingdom.

2. Seeking the Kingdom of God

Seeking the Kingdom of God and His righteousness should be a first priority for the Christian. Paul states in the book of Romans that the Kingdom is in the Holy Spirit. Therefore, to seek the Kingdom is to seek the ways and leadership of the Spirit in the activities of our lives. Righteousness is the character of the Spirit. Peace is the result of following the Spirit, and joy defines the attitude of those in the Kingdom.

<u>Matthew 6:33</u> – But seek first the kingdom of God and His righteousness, and all these things will be added to you.

<u>Romans 14:17</u> – for the kingdom of God is not eating and drinking, but righteousness and peace and joy in the Holy Spirit.

<u>John 16:13</u> – However, when He, the Spirit of truth, has come, He will guide you into all truth; for He will not speak on His own authority but whatever He hears He will speak; and He will tell you things to come.

Seeking the Kingdom of God is discovering its principles, truths, and attributes under the leading of the Holy Spirit, and applying these truths in our lives (Matthew 4:4). Seeking the Kingdom is constantly acquiring knowledge and application of its principles. Therefore, we must seek to understand its truths little by little or by precept upon precept. This process is called renewing the mind and is a life long process.

- <u>II Peter 1:5-8</u> – But also for this very reason, giving all diligence, add to your faith virtue, to virtue knowledge, (6) to knowledge self-control, to self-control perseverance, to perseverance godliness, (7) to godliness brotherly kindness, and to brotherly kindness love, (8) For if these things are yours and abound, you will be neither barren nor unfruitful in the knowledge of our Lord Jesus Christ. (9) For he who lacks these things is shortsighted, even to blindness, and has forgotten that he was cleansed from his old sins.

The Christian maturing process is summarized in these scriptures. Verses five, six, and seven contained the attributes essential to the process of spiritual growth. Each attribute is necessary for maintaining a holistic Christian lifestyle. Each attribute represents a principle of the Kingdom. They provide the proper Christian response to daily life encounters and situations. Verse eight promises fruitfulness and increased knowledge of Jesus to those who apply these attributes. Verse nine describes the person who fails to apply these attributes in his life. This list is not a sequence; each attribute has its on merits.

The Christian is confronted with thoughts, issues, decisions, and situations that challenge each of these attributes. The manner in which he responds to these challenges has a direct effect on his spiritual growth. Individuals who seek the ways of the Kingdom will consider these attributes as guideposts to aid them in their spiritual walk.

Romans chapter 12:2 admonishes Christians to not be conformed to this world, but be transformed by the renewing of their mind. The process in II Peter 1:5-7 gives guidelines on how to guard against conforming to worldly temptations and issues. For example, during our day we face numerous situations that oppose one or more of these attributes. We encounter situations that challenge our faith or Christian morals. When we exercise faith, and choose a virtuous response we resist the world, flesh, and the devil. This is also true of the attributes of acquiring godly knowledge, self-control, perseverance, godliness, brotherly kindness, and biblical love. Therefore, to seek God's Kingdom is the acquiring and application of biblical knowledge.

3. Life of the Kingdom

Kingdom life is a supernatural life. Jesus is the only source of eternal life. This life is a supernatural life that provides the individual with grace and power. A person must be born again spiritually to possess eternal life, and fully express the principles of the Kingdom. The greatest decision a person can make during his life time is to trust Jesus as savior. To reject the Son of God is to reject eternal life and forfeit the grace gospel of the Kingdom.

Paul describes the attitude of those who reject Christ in Romans 1:16-32. The rich young ruler also rejected eternal life for earthly riches. (Matthew 19:16-22). He chose temporary wealth and comfort over heaven and eternal life. Sadly, many still choose worldly things over the true treasures of the Kingdom. A man may sacrifice his soul for wealth, and lose it or die and leave it to someone else. (Luke 12:16-21). The person who believes in Jesus chooses the supernatural life of His Kingdom.

The Holy Spirit anointed Jesus at the beginning of His earthly ministry (Matthew 3:16–4:1). After enduring the temptations of the devil in the wilderness, He began to preach about the Kingdom. He demonstrated characteristics of the Kingdom through miracles, healings, compassion, and love.

Jesus taught His disciples that when He went back to heaven the Holy Spirit would come to indwell them. He would guide and empower them. Before He ascended back to heaven He instructed them to wait in Jerusalem until He sent the Holy Spirit. He assured them the Holy Spirit would give them power to be His witnesses in the world. When He ascended to the right hand of the Father He released the Holy Spirit on the day of Pentecost.

Acts 1:4 – And being assembled together with them, He commanded them not to depart from Jerusalem, but to wait for the Promise of the Father, 'which", He said, "you have heard from Me;

Acts 1:8 – But you shall receive power when the Holy Spirit has come upon you; and you shall be witnesses to Me in Jerusalem, and in all Judea and Samaria, and to the end of the earth.

Acts 2:1 – When the Day of Pentecost had fully come, they were all with one accord in one place.

Acts 2:33 – Therefore being exalted to the right hand of God, and having received from the Father the promise of the Holy Spirit, He poured out this which you now see and hear.

John 16:7-14 –Nevertheless I tell you the truth. It is to your advantage that I go away; for if I do not go away, the Helper will not come to you; but if I depart, I will send Him to you (8) And when He has come, He will convict the world of sin, and of righteousness, and of judgment: (9) of sin, because they do not believe in Me; (10) of righteousness, because I go to My Father and you see Me no more; (11) of judgment, because the ruler of this world is judged. (12) I still have many things to say to you, but you cannot bear them now. (13) However, when He, the Spirit of truth, has come, He will guide you into all truth; for He will not speak on His own authority, but whatever He hears He will speak; and He will tell you things to come. (14) He will glorify Me, for He will take what is Mine and declare it to you.

This is the essence of life in the Kingdom.

CHAPTER FIVE

Exploring the grace of God

The word "grace" is used in a general manner throughout the Christian and worldly communities. This has caused the significance of its true meaning to become obscured or altogether lost. Grace is the very essence of the gospel. Regardless of how it is administered it is pure in motive, attitude, and action. It has no negative qualities, no down side, or adverse effects. Grace is the key to understanding the gospel, and the Kingdom of God. Therefore, it is essential for every believer to have a true understanding of what it means to be a beneficiary of God's grace. When a person grasps the scope of biblical grace it may conflict with some doctrines he has previously embraced. To practice grace will cause a person to adjust his beliefs and paradigms.

Throughout the generations of Christianity the Holy Spirit has used men and movements to emphasize a neglected or greater aspect of the Kingdom. Currently I believe the Spirit's emphasis is on the Kingdom of God and the gospel of grace. Although grace was an emphasis in the time of Paul, and the early church it has lost its biblical significance in many modern churches. The clear lines between the law and grace have become so intertwined that the purity of the gospel of grace has been compromised.

The Holy Spirit never emphasizes one thing to the neglect of other equally important attributes of the Kingdom. Wherever grace is emphasized it will always include such things as worship, giving, forgiveness, righteousness, love, and evangelism. The teaching of grace will never weaken the old tried doctrines of the faith.

A major factor in understanding grace is being able to separate the requirements of the Old and New Covenants. The Christian bible is divided into two parts, the Old Testament, and the New Testament. These represent the two major covenants which God established with men. One is a covenant of laws, and the other is a covenant of grace. The bible records how God relates to men under each of these covenants. One covenant supersedes the other, and their requirements can not be mixed.

The requirements of the Old Covenant were given to Moses by God on Mount Sinai while the Israelites were in the wilderness. This covenant was a composite of laws consisting of 613 requirements. It included the Ten Commandments, dietary laws, moral laws, civil laws and sacrificial laws. These are often referred to in the scriptures as the "Law". The contents of this covenant were the basis of Israel's relationship with God. It contained both blessings and curses. Their obedience to the laws determined which they received.

In the same manner the New Covenant is a composite of God grace. It includes every way God reveals His goodness to mankind. The noun "grace" identifies every good attribute of God. This includes His love, mercy, kindness, forgiveness, provisions, protection, healing, and every benevolent act. The verb "grace" identifies the individual expressions of His goodness. Grace is God's goodness in action. For example, God's love is His grace activated. Grace is any manifestation of God goodness to individuals. Anytime we experience the goodness of God in any manner we are experiencing His grace. When we express these same attributes to others we are sharing God's grace.

Two major purposes of God's grace to mankind are redeeming grace, and enabling grace. One includes everything that God has done to redeem fallen man. The other outlines the individual responsibilities of those who have been redeemed. One focuses on God's love for man, the other focuses on man's love for God. Not understanding these differences has caused confusions among Christians.

(a) Redeeming grace: Redeeming grace includes God's original purpose for creating man in His image. It contains the fall of Adam and the sacrifices God made to restore man to His original purpose.

God's plan for the redemption of mankind was conceived by the Trinity before the foundation of the world. This plan was consummated by Jesus, the Son of God. He came to earth and revealed the heart of God, the Father. He lived a perfect sinless life and died on the cross as the substitute for all mankind. His death secured the forgiveness of man's sin. He was raised from the dead and ascended back to heaven. In heaven He performed His duties as High Priest and sat down at the right hand of the Father to intercede for believers.

When Jesus died on the cross He took the punishment for every sin from the beginning to the end of time. The penalty for sin was death and Jesus paid that penalty for all of mankind. This reconciled man to God which allows him the choice to believe in Jesus for eternal life

With His last breath Jesus declared from the cross, "It is finished". Perhaps man will never know all that Jesus meant when He made that declaration. But, His sacrifice made all the blessings of the gospel of grace available to us. The following are a few:

- God's plan for the redemption of mankind is completed. God has reconciled man to Himself. Therefore, it is now man's choice to believe in God's Son and receive eternal life, or to reject Him and go to hell.
    - II Corinthians 5:19 –That is, that God was in Christ reconciling the world to Himself, not imputing their trespasses to them, and has committed to us the word of reconciliation.
    - John 6:40 – And this is the will of Him who sent Me, that everyone who sees the Son and believes in Him may have everlasting life; and I will raise him up at the last day.
    - John 3:16 – for God so loved the world that He gave His only begotten Son, that whoever believes in Him should not perish but have everlasting life.

- God's wrath toward mankind is satisfied and He is not angry with men.
    - Romans 5:9 – Much more then, having now been justified by His blood, we shall be saved from wrath through Him.

- The punishment for sin has been satisfied and God has forgiven mankind for their sins.
    - I John 2:2 - And He Himself is the propitiation for our sins, and not for ours only but also for the whole world.

- God forgives all sins and forgets them.
    - Hebrews 10:17 – then He adds, "Their sins and their lawless deeds I will remember no more.

- Curses associated with the law are removed and only blessing remain.
    - Galatians 3:13 – Christ has redeemed us from the curse of the law, having become a curse for us (for it is written, "Cursed is everyone who hangs on a tree")
    - II Corinthians 1:20 – For all the promises of God in Him are Yes, and in Him Amen, to the glory of God through us.

- We are no longer alienated from God.
    - II Corinthians 5:18 – Now all things are of God, who has reconciled us to Himself through Jesus Christ, and has given us the ministry of reconciliation.

- We are acceptable to God, and no longer have to perform to be accepted.
    - Ephesians 1:6 – to the praise of the glory of His grace, by which He made us accepted in the beloved.

- Those who believe are placed into God.
    - John 14:20 – At that day you will know that I am in My Father, and you in Me, and I in you.
    - I Corinthians 12:13 – for by one Spirit we were all baptized into one body – whether Jews or Greeks, whether slaves or free – and have all been made to drink into one Spirit.

- Our spirit and God's Spirit become one.
  - I Corinthians 6:17 But he who is joined to the Lord is one spirit with Him.

- God promises to provide everything we need for life and godliness.
  - II Peter 1:3 – As His divine power has given to us all things that pertain to life and godliness, through the knowledge of Him who called us by glory and virtue.

- Believers become part of God's family and enjoy a relationship with Him.
  - John 1:12 – But as many as received Him, to them He gave the right to become children of God, to those who believe in His name.

- Christians are joint heirs with Christ.
  - Romans 8:17 – and if children, then heirs- heirs of God and joint heirs with Christ, if indeed we suffer with Him, that we may also be glorified together.

This is not an exhaustive list of what He meant when He said "it is finished". These and many more are included by grace under the New Covenant.

This is the redeeming grace of God. Jesus declares with His last breath that His purpose is finished. Everything needed for the redemption of mankind has been completed. Grace is made available so individuals can receive salvation. God has done it all! Man can not add or take away anything from it. Individuals must believe in God's Son to have access to all these gracelets.

(b). Enabling Grace: Enabling grace is the grace that God provides through the ministry of the Holy Spirit that enables us to mature as Christians and assume our responsibilities in the Kingdom of God.

- <u>Acts 1:8</u> – But you shall receive power when the Holy Spirit has come upon you; and you shall be witnesses to Me in Jerusalem, and in all Judea and Samaria, and to the end of the world.
- <u>Ephesians 2:10</u> – For we are His workmanship created in Christ Jesus for good works, which God prepared beforehand that we should walk in them.
- <u>Philippians 2:13</u> – for it is God who works in you both to will and to do for His good pleasure
- <u>Philippians 1:6</u> – Being confident of this very thing, that He who has begun a good work in you will complete it until the day of Jesus Christ.
- <u>II Corinthians 5:18-19</u> – Now all things are of God, who has reconciled us to Himself through Jesus Christ, and has given us the ministry of reconciliation. (19) that is, that God was in Christ reconciling the world to Himself not imputing their trespasses to them, and has committed to us the word of reconciliation.

Redeeming grace provides a person with the knowledge and faith to be born spiritually and receive eternal life. Enabling grace provides the person with the power and guidance to live as responsible subjects in the Kingdom of God. Grace enables Christians to live as God's representatives in a manner that will draw men to believe in Him and possess eternal life

- Romans 12:9-21 outlines how a life in grace should look.

CHAPTER SIX

The Old Covenant versus the New Covenant

The importance of covenant is stressed by the number of times it is mention in the bible. It occurs 280 times in the Old Testament and 33 times in the New Testament. God relates to His people through covenants. The bible records covenants between individuals, a king and his subjects, and God and individuals. Covenants can be conditional or unconditional. If a covenant is conditional and one of the parties violates it, the terms of the covenant are forfeited. If the covenant is unconditional the violation of one party does not negate the fulfillment of its terms.

The Hebrew word covenant is "Beriyth" which implies the procedure of cutting a covenant. The covenant is made by individuals passing between the cut pieces of the flesh of a slain animal (Genesis 15:17-18; Jeremiah 34:18) In the New Testament the Greek word for God initiated covenants is "Diatheke". This is a legal term denoting a formal and legally binding declaration of benefits to be given by one party to another, with or without conditions attached.

In modern times covenant has lost its significance. But, in biblical times it was the solemn means for men to commit themselves to each other for various reasons. God made covenants with individuals and a nation. He still relates to His people through covenant. The New Covenant is God's current covenant with Christians. If a person is not in covenant with God he does not have a relationship with God.

The Old Covenant was between God and Abraham's descendants. God gave Moses the conditions of the covenant on Mt. Sinai while Israel was in the wilderness. It was written by God on tablets of stone. It never applied to any other nation. It was initiated on the first Pentecost after they left Egypt and consisted of 613 different laws. It was a conditional covenant. God's benevolent acts were in direct proportion to Israel's adherence to the conditions of covenant. The Old Covenant was terminated by God and replaced with the New Covenant following the resurrection of Jesus.

Exodus 31:18 – And when He had made an end of speaking with him on Mount Sinai, He gave Moses two tablets of the Testimony, tablets of stone, written with the finger of God

Hebrews 8:10 – For this is the covenant that I will make with the house of Israel after those days, says the Lord: I will put My laws in their mind and write them on their hearts; and I will be their God, and they shall be My people.

Hebrews 8:13 – In that He says, "A new covenant," He has made the first obsolete. Now what is becoming obsolete and growing old is ready to vanish away.

Under the Old Covenant priests and Levites were appointed. They offered animal sacrifices for sin, received tithes from the people, and maintained the tabernacle and temple of worship. The Old Covenant was a composite of the Ten Commandments, dietary, civil, moral, and sacrificial laws that Israel was responsible to keep. Sins were forgiven through the sacrifices of animals. It contained blessings and curses. Blessings when they obeyed the law and curses when they did not. (Deuteronomy 28:1-68 (14 verses of blessings, 54 of curses)

The apostle Paul refers to this covenant as a ministry of death and condemnation because no one was able to keep its strict requirements. The Israelites were violating the conditions of the covenant even while Moses was receiving them from God. Three thousand died as the result of their violation.

Exodus 32:25-28 – Now when Moses saw that the people were unrestrained (for Aaron had not restrained them, to their shame among their enemies). (26) Then Moses stood in the entrance of the camp, and said, "Whoever is on the Lord's side – come to me!" And all the sons of Levi gathered themselves together to him. (27) And he said to them, "Thus says the Lord God of Israel: "Let every man put his sword on his side, and go in and out from entrance to entrance throughout the camp, and let every man kill his brother, every man his companion, and every man his neighbor." (28) So the sons of Levi did according to the word of Moses. And about three thousand men of the people fell that day

II Corinthians 3:6-8 – Who also made us sufficient as ministers of the new covenant, not of the letter but of the Spirit; for the letter kills, but the Spirit gives life (7) But if the ministry of death, written and engraved on stones, was glorious, so that the children of Israel could not look steadily at the face of Moses because of the glory of his countenance, which glory was passing away, (8) how will the ministry of the Spirit not be more glorious.

II Corinthians 3:9 – For if the ministry of condemnation had glory, the ministry of righteousness exceeds much more in glory. (Comparing the two covenants)

The laws of the Old Covenant were given so that God's people could identify acts and attitudes of sin. They revealed that it is impossible to maintain a relationship with a Holy God by attempting to follow a set of laws. No manner of performance can achieve the righteousness required by God. This dilemma was solved by the establishment of the New Covenant.

Ezekiel 20:25 – Therefore I also gave them up to statutes that were not good, and judgments by which they could not live.

Galatians 3:10- for as many as are of the works of the law are under the curse; for it is written, "Cursed is everyone who does not continue in all things which are written in the book of the law, to do them.

James 2:10 – For whoever shall keep the whole law, and yet stumble in one point, he is guilty of all.

The Old Covenant was terminated by God. The New Covenant was initiated on the first Pentecost after the death and resurrection of Jesus. Three thousand souls were saved bearing evidence that this was a superior covenant.

Acts 2:1 – When the Day of Pentecost had full come, they were all with one accord in one place.

Acts 2:41 – Then those who gladly received his word were baptized; and that day about three thousand souls were added to them

Hebrews 8:6-8 –But now He has obtained a more excellent ministry, inasmuch as He is also a Mediator of a better covenant, which was established on better promises. (7) For if that first covenant had been faultless, then no place would have been sought for a second. (8) Because finding fault with them, He says; "Behold, the days are coming, says the Lord, when I will make a new covenant with the house of Israel and with the house of Judah.

Hebrews 8:13 –In that He says, "A new covenant," He has made the first obsolete. Now what is becoming obsolete and growing old is ready to vanish away.

Note: Although the Old Covenant applied to Israel alone it stills contains many treasures and guidelines that are valuable for the Christian. The tabernacle, feast days, Ark of the Covenant, and mercy seat were all pictures of Jesus. Many of the things recorded in the Old Testament were shadows of things that were fulfilled in the New Testament. They are important in understanding the New Testament writings. But it is foolish to hold on to the shadows and try to incorporate them into our doctrines when we have the true substance in Christ.

Major differences of the New Covenant of Grace:

- It is a covenant between the Father and the Son and can not be broken.

  Galatians 3:16 – Now to Abraham and his Seed were the promises made. He does not say, "And to seeds," as of many, but as of one, "And to your Seed", who is Christ.

  Hebrews 8:6 – But now He has obtained a more excellent ministry, inasmuch as He is also Mediator of a better covenant, which was established on better promises.

  Hebrews 9:24 – For Christ has not entered the holy places made with hands, which are copies of the true, but into heaven itself, now to appear in the presence of God for us.

  Hebrews 12:24 – to Jesus the Mediator of the new covenant, and to the blood of sprinkling that speaks better things than that of Abel

- It includes all believers.

  John 1:12 – But as many as received Him, to them He gave the right to become children of God, to those who believe in His name.
- Begins when the believer is placed into the body of Christ.

I Corinthians 12:13 – for by one Spirit we were all baptized into one body – whether Jews or Greeks, whether slaves of free – and have all been made to drink into one Spirit.

- It is a covenant of grace with Jesus as provider.

  John 1:16-17 – And of His fullness we have all received, and grace for grace. (17) For the law was given through Moses but grace and truth came through Jesus Christ.
- Is written on the heart of believers.

  Hebrews 8:10 - For this is the covenant that I will make with the house of Israel after those days, says the Lord: I will put My laws in their mind and write them on their hearts; and I will be their God, and they shall be My people.
- All believers are priests.

  1 Peter 2:5 – you also, as living stones, are being built up a spiritual house, a holy priesthood, to offer up spiritual sacrifices acceptable to God through Jesus Christ.

  1 Peter 2:9 – But you are a chosen generation, a royal priesthood, a holy nation, His own special people, that you may proclaim the praises of Him who called you out of darkness into His marvelous light;
- God's temple is the body of believers.

  1 Corinthians 6:19 – Or do you not know that your body is the temple of the Holy Spirit who is in you, whom you have from God, and you are not your own?
- It was ratified on the first Pentecost after Jesus' crucifixion when the Holy Spirit was poured out, and 3,000 souls were saved.

  Acts 2:1-4 –When the Day of Pentecost had fully come, they were all with one accord in one place. (2) And suddenly there came a sound from heaven, as of a rushing might wind, and it filled the whole house where they were sitting. (3) Then there appeared to them divided tongues, as of fire, and one sat upon each of them. (4) And they were all filled with the Holy Spirit and began to speak with other tongues, as the Spirit gave them utterance.

Acts 2:33 – Therefore being exalted to the right hand of God, and having received from the Father the promise of the Holy Spirit, He poured out this which you now see and hear.

Acts 2:41 – Then those who gladly received his word were baptized; and that day about three thousand souls were added to them.

- The Holy Spirit provides the Christian with the power and guidance to be effective ministers of the gospel of grace.

Acts 1:8 – But you shall receive power when the Holy Spirit has come upon you; and you shall be witnesses to Me in Jerusalem, and in all Judea and Samaria, and to the end of the earth.

John 16:13 – However, when He, the Spirit of truth, has come, He will guide you into all truth; for He will not speak on His own authority, but whatever He hears He will speak; and He will tell you things to come.

- Replaced the Old Covenant of law

Hebrews 8:6-13 – But now He has obtained a more excellent ministry, inasmuch as He is also Mediator of a better covenant, which was established on better promises. (7) For if that first covenant had been faultless, then no place would be sought for a second. (8) Because finding fault with them, He says: "Behold, the days are coming, says the Lord, when I will make a new covenant with the house of Israel ad with the house of Judah. (13) In that He says, "A new covenant," He has made the first obsolete. Now what is becoming obsolete and growing old is ready to vanish away.

The Benefits of the New Covenant:

1. Makes us a member of God's family – John 1:12, Romans 8:14-17
2. Provides us with everything we need for life and godliness – II Peter 1:3

3. Provides righteousness as a gift not as a performance – II Corinthians 5:21, Romans 5:17
4. Frees us from all condemnation of the Law – Romans 8:1-4
5. Frees us from the punishment and power of sin – Romans 6:14, I Corinthians 6:11, Hebrews 10:17
6. Makes us saints and not sinners – I Corinthians 1:2, Hebrews 10:10,14
7. Makes all the promises in Him yes – II Corinthians 1:20
8. Provides us with eternal security by the sealing of the Holy Spirit – I Corinthians 1:22, Ephesians 4:30
9. Is a covenant with blessings only and no curses – Galatians 3:13
10. It is superior to the law in that it provides life not death, acceptance not condemnation.

CHAPTER SEVEN

Developing our identity with Christ

Identity is the personality or individual character traits that distinguish one person from all others. It also means exact likeness in nature or qualities. Jesus was the exact likeness of the Father.

A person's identity is developed by a compilation of psychological and social factors. It is influenced by what he is exposed to in his formative years; the culture in which he lives, family and friends, and the many factors of the world in which he lives. It also includes the image that he has of himself.

What a person believes about himself dictates his actions, interests, creativity, values, beliefs, choices, and relationships. How a person views himself influences his decisions, attitude, self-worth, confidence, and general view of his world. When identity is based on performance, abilities, education, looks, or others appraisals it will always be a distorted image.

There are three major influences that contribute to a person developing a wrong image of himself. These are the devil, the world system, and the human flesh. The devil is the archenemy of God. He will do anything to distort the identity of those created in God's image to prevent them reaching their full potential and purpose. The world system consists of opposing philosophies, religions, and ideologies. It attempts to shape one's identity by opposing or contradicting the truths, morals, and values taught in the bible. The flesh is that unconverted entity within us that aligns itself with the devil and the world to establish an identity compatible with it desires.

The Christian's only means of attaining his true identity is to believe what he sees in the mirror of the scriptures (James 1:23-25). The new birth places us in Christ and we assume His likeness. The scriptures states "as He is, so are we in this world (I John 4:17). The Christian is constantly upgrading his identity by renewing his mind to accept the positive attributes he sees in the bible.

When a person believes in Jesus Christ his human spirit is born again with a divine nature which is his true identity. A person exercises his true identity by allowing this new nature to direct his activities and attitudes. Many Christians believe they must do all manner of religious works to become the person they see described in the Scriptures. In reality a Christian performs good works because he already has a new nature, not to become a better person. Christians are created in the image of God and their identity should be formed from this truth.

Christians whose identity is derived from their association with God will resist the devil, world, and flesh. They will not allow the lack or attainment of their position in society, educational level, or abilities, to influence them away from their true identity in Christ.

The image we have of ourselves governs our behavior. Changing our image to how God sees us will cause a positive change in our behavior. The process of renewing the mind is the act of adjusting our paradigms and beliefs to what the Holy Spirits teaches us from the bible.

Romans 12:2 – And do not be conformed to this world, but be transformed by the renewing of your mind, that you may prove what is that good and acceptable and perfect will of God.

Matthew 4:17 – From that time Jesus began to preach and to say, repent, for the kingdom of heaven is at hand

Mark 1:15 – and saying "The time is fulfilled, and the kingdom of God is at hand. Repent and believe in the gospel

The true meaning of repentance is to change the way we think so that it causes a change in our actions and attitudes. True repentance is the first step in renewing the mind. A renewed mind embraces the biblical image of who we are in Christ.

How the bible defines the Christian:

1. We are a child of God
    - Romans 8:16 – The Spirit Himself bears witness with our spirit that we are children of God
    - John 1:12 - But as many as received Him, to them He gave the right to become children of God, to those who believe in His name.

2. We have a divine nature.
    - II Peter 1:4 – By which have been given to us exceedingly great and precious promises, that through these you may be partakers of the divine nature, having escaped the corruption that is in the world through lust.
    - I Corinthians 6:17 – But he who is joined to the Lord is one spirit with Him.

3. We are the righteousness of God.
    - II Corinthians 5:21 –For He made Him who knew no sin to be sin for us, that we might become the righteousness of God in Him.
    - Romans 3:22 – Even the righteousness of
    - God, through faith in Jesus Christ, to all and on all who believe. For there is no difference.
    - - Romans 5:17 – For if by the one man's offense death reigned through the one, much more those who receive abundance of grace and of the gift of righteousness will reign in life through the One, Jesus Christ.

4. We are saints not sinners.
    - I Corinthians 1:2 –To the church of God which is a Corinth, to those who are called to be saints, with all who in every place call on the name of Jesus.

5. We are joint heirs with Christ.
    - Romans 8:17 – and if children, then heirs –heirs of God and joint heirs with Christ

- II Peter 1:3 As His divine power has given to us all things that pertain to life and godliness.
- II Corinthians 1:20 – for all the promises of God in Him are Yes, and in Him Amen.

6. We are forever secure in Him.
    - Ephesians 4:30 – And do not grieve the Holy Spirit of God, by whom you were sealed for the day of redemption.
    - II Corinthians 1:22 – who also has sealed us and given us the Spirit in our hearts as a guarantee.

7. The glory of God is upon us.
    - John 17:22 – and the glory which You gave Me I have given them, that they may be one just as we are one.

We must believe what God says is true and adjust our lives to embrace these truths.

> James 1:22 – 25 – But be doers of the word, and not hearers only, deceiving yourselves. (23) for if anyone is a hearer of the word and not a doer, he is like a man observing his natural face in a mirror. (24) For he observes himself, goes away, and immediately forgets what kind of man he was (25) But he who looks into the perfect law of liberty (grace gospel) and continues in it, and is not a forgetful hearer but a doer of the work, this one will be blessed in what he does.

God sees us as He designed us to be: beautiful, intelligent, full of wisdom, creative, and righteous. Don't let the devil or others deceive you into believing that you are anything less than who God says you are.

CHAPTER EIGHT

Renewing of the Mind

The human mind is the faculty through which a person thinks, imagines, remembers, perceives, reasons, judges, recognizes, and processes data. The stored data of the mind is the basis of forming the paradigms that govern our lives. We are constantly altering or reinforcing these paradigms by the experiences and data we are exposed to daily.

A paradigm is a set of acquired beliefs, philosophies, laws, disciplines, standards, and behavioral patterns. These govern every aspect of our lives. We also base our security on going to heaven on these beliefs. Paradigms also include our comfort zones and defense mechanisms. Many of our paradigms are formed from worldly data that conflict with biblical truths and practices. When a person becomes a Christian he must adjust his beliefs to align with his new nature. This is known as renewing the mind.

Renewing the mind is the life long process of a person adjusting his thinking to align with biblical truths as revealed by the Holy Spirit. Biblical repentance is a major factor in renewing the mind.

The New Testament meaning of repentance is a change that affects the heart and mind which leads to a change of behavior. Jesus states that to repent is to believe the gospel (Mark 1:14-15) He was referring to the good news of His Kingdom that He taught and demonstrated during His earthly ministry.

True repentance occurs when a person realizes his actions, attitude, or thoughts are biblically wrong and changes them. The renewing of the mind is the first step to repentance. It causes a person to change his behavior and actions by changing his paradigms.

The paradigms of Israel were formed by living under the requirements of the laws of Moses. They were also influenced by the teachings of the Pharisees and Sadducees. Many religious practices had arisen during the prior four hundred years when there were no prophets of God to guide the people. The things that Jesus taught and demonstrated were new and different. Jesus' message was about the good news of a new kingdom that He likens to new wine. Just like new wine requires new wineskins the gospel requires people to think differently.

Understanding how paradigms are formed is helpful in renewing the mind. A person does not have to be a student of neuroscience or psychology to have a general idea about the function of the brain. The ingenuity of the human brain is evidence of the creativity of God. The brain is constantly recording, cataloging, and storing data. It receives this data through the five senses, i.e., sight, hearing, taste, touch, and smell. Although it may not be scientific, lets suppose that the brain stores this data in different compartments. These compartments correspond to the five senses and the soul. The soul consists of the mind, will and emotions. We are able to identify certain sights, sounds, tastes, objects, and smells that are common in our world because they have been identified and recorded by our brain.

The brain is able to recall and define facts learned years ago and use these facts in current situations. The brain also stores a wide spectrum of emotions as we interact with the world around us.

The brain uses the information stored in these compartments to direct our decisions and responses in life activities. When we encounter a situation the brain analyses the situation based upon stored data. For example, you are walking through a wooded area and hear a rattling sound. Your brain instantly analyses from its data that the sound is associated with a rattlesnake. The brain then dictates which action to take, stand very still or jump and run. This gathering of stored data is what forms the paradigms of our lives.

The brain is constantly upgrading the data stored in these compartments with new learned data. It is easily understood that in order to change our actions we must change the data stored in the brain. This is also true of the biblical concept of renewing the mind. The data stored in our brain must be corrected or replaced by accepting biblical truths revealed by the Holy Spirit.

The purpose of studying the bible is to acquire data that governs our relationship with God and others. The data we receive from the bible is of a spiritual nature. It may resonate as truth in our spirit without being verified by the stored data of the brain. Faith is an example.

The bible encourages us to not be conformed to this world, but to be transformed by the renewing of our mind, that we may prove what is the good and acceptable and perfect will of God (Romans 12:2). When Jesus was in the wilderness tempted by the devil He gave us the key to successful Christian living, and defeating the devil. It is by following His instruction that our mind is renewed.

Matthew 4:4 – But He answered and said, "It is written, 'Man shall not live by bread alone, but by every word that proceeds from the mouth of God'.

- Every sincere Christian realizes that everything God says to him is important.
- The underlying truth of this verse is a person must actively listen to God.
- God speaks personally to an individual concerning those things that are pertinent to his life.
- The words that God speak provide essential guidance in all areas of a person's life.
- God's words are both spiritual and life (John 6:63).
- He will always provide the grace and ability to respond to His instructions (Philippians 2:13)
- The key to the Christian life is actively listening to God and applying what He tells us in our lives.

The renewing of the mind replaces a person's thoughts, beliefs, and paradigms with the truths he receives by listening to God. His outward behavior will conform to these new truths. This may also be referred to as, "growing in grace and the knowledge of God".

Repentance is constantly adjusting of our thinking and actions to align with the truths revealed to us by the Holy Spirit from the Word of God. This process continues throughout the Christian's life.

After Jesus had ascended to heaven He sent the Holy Spirit to tutor Christians in the ways of the Kingdom of God, and empower them to live as children of God.

John 16:7 – Nevertheless I tell you the truth. It is to your advantage that I go away; for if I do not go away, the Helper will not come to you; but if I depart, I will send Him to you.

John 16:13 – However, when He, the Spirit of truth, has come, He will guide you into all truth, for He will not speak on His own authority but whatever He hears He will speak; and He will tell you things to come.

- We have the assurance and comfort that the Holy Spirit will lead us into all truth and provide guidance for our future.
- Romans 8:14-15 – For as many as are led by the Spirit of God, these are the sons of God. (15) For you did not receive the spirit of bondage again to fear, but you received the Spirit of adoption by whom we cry out, "Abba, Father."

CHAPTER NINE

Growing in grace and the knowledge of God

Many Christians can relate to the Apostle Peter. We can recall those times when we allowed the fear of man to cause us to deny our relationship with Jesus. We know the joy of being forgiven a grievous sin. We understand the honor of being trusted with a leadership position. Jesus forgave Peter for his denial and appointed him to "feed My sheep". A responsibility Peter took very seriously. His letters contain instructions, encouragement, and guide lines that address the welfare of his sheep. Peter sums up his letters with perhaps one of the greatest goals a Christian can pursue.

II Peter 3:18 – "But grow in the grace and knowledge of our Lord and Savior Jesus Christ. To Him be the glory both now and forever. Amen".

Grow: In the understanding and application of grace by acquiring knowledge of Jesus Christ. Acquired knowledge becomes experiential knowledge when it is exercised through grace.

Knowledge: Biblical truths as revealed by the Holy Spirit.

I Peter 2:2 – As newborn babes, desire the pure milk of the word, that you may grow thereby.

- Colossians 1:10 – that you may walk worthy of the Lord, fully pleasing Him, being fruitful in every good work and increasing in the knowledge (gnosis) of God

Knowledge: The Greek words for knowledge are: "Gnosis" which means seeking to know, an enquiry, investigation of spiritual truth, and "Ginosko" meaning to take in knowledge, to come to know, recognize, understand. In the New Testament

"Ginosko" frequently indicates a relation between the person "knowing" and the object known; in this respect, what is "known" is of value or importance to the one who knows, especially of God's knowledge. Such "knowledge" is obtained, not by mere intellectual activity, but by revelation from the Holy Spirit. When used as a verb it means to know by observation and experience. Examples:

II Peter 3:18 – but grow in the grace and knowledge (Gnosis - continuous acquiring of knowledge of Jesus) of our Lord and Savior Jesus Christ.

II Peter 1:5, But also for this reason, giving all diligence, add to your faith virtue, to virtue knowledge_(Gnosis = developing knowledge in each of these areas)

Another Greek word for knowledge is "Epignosis" meaning the complete comprehension that comes from a full understanding of the gathered knowledge (gnosis). Something that was barely known before is now more familiar; a more exact understanding of a subject previously not fully understood. The small portions of knowledge (gnosis) is improved upon and it is seen more strongly and clearly: a knowledge that allows for greater participation by the "knower" in the object "known" thus more powerfully influencing him.

The Greek word "Epiginosko" means to become fully acquainted with, fully perceive, discern, recognize, to the point of it becoming a part of one's paradigm. The following are examples of the use of the word knowledge:

- Romans 1:32 – Who, knowing (epiginosko) the righteous judgment of God, that those who practice such things are deserving of death, not only do the same but also approve of those who practice them.
- I Corinthians 13:12 – for now we see in a mirror, dimly, but then face to face. Now I know (ginosko) in part, but then I shall know (epiginosko) just as I also am known.

II Peter 1:2 – Grace and peace be multiplied to you in the knowledge (ginosko) of God and of Jesus our Lord

II Peter 1:3 – As His divine power has given to us all things that pertain to life and godliness, through the knowledge (epignosis) of Him who called us by glory and virtue.

II Peter 1:8 –For if these things are yours and abound, you will be neither barren nor unfruitful in the knowledge (epignosis) of our Lord Jesus Christ.

II Peter 2:20 – For if, after they have escaped the pollutions of the world through the knowledge (epignosis) of the Lord and Savior Jesus Christ, they are again entangled in them and overcome, the latter end is worse for them than the beginning.

The Greek word "Agnosia" means an ignorance of the knowledge of God. This includes those who call themselves agnostics because they confess no experiential knowledge of God. It also includes all false religions, cults and occults around the world.

- I Corinthians 15:34 – Awake to righteousness, and do not sin; for some do not have the knowledge (Agnosia) of God. I speak this to your shame."

Knowledge of God: Knowledge that God has revealed about Himself, His Kingdom, and His grace.

Matthew 11:29 – Take My yoke upon you and learn from Me, for I am gentle and lowly in heart, and you will find rest for your souls."

Romans 11:33 – Oh, the depth of the riches both of the wisdom and knowledge (ginosko) of God! How unsearchable are His judgments and His ways past finding out!

Ephesians 1:17 – That the God of our Lord Jesus Christ, the Father of glory, may give to you the spirit of wisdom and revelation in the knowledge (ginosko) of Him.

Ephesians 4:13 – Till we all come to the unity of the faith and of the knowledge (ginosko) of the Son of God, to a perfect man, to the measure of the stature of the fullness of Christ.

In the garden Adam and Eve had the choice of acquiring knowledge of God or the knowledge of good and evil. They made the wrong choice as many still do.

Romans 10:2 – For I bear them witness that they have a zeal for God, but not according to knowledge (ginosko).

How we can receive this knowledge:

I Peter 1:3 – As His divine power has given to us all things that pertain to life and godliness, through the knowledge of Him who called us by glory and virtue.

I Corinthians 2:9 - But as it is written; eye has not seen, nor ear heard, nor have entered into the heart of man, the things which God has prepared for those who love Him.

I Corinthians 2:10 – But God has revealed them to us through His Spirit.

Romans 10:17 – So then faith come by hearing, and hearing by the word of God.

Matthew 4:4 – But He answered and said, "it is written, Man shall not live by bread alone, but by every word that proceeds from the mouth of God.

John 6:63 – It is the Spirit who gives life; the flesh profits nothing. The words that I speak to you are spirit, and they are life."

John 16:12 – I still have many things to say to you, but you cannot bear them now.

John 16:13 – However, when He, the Spirit of truth, has come, He will guide you into all truth; for He will not speak on His own authority, but whatever He hears He will speak; and He will tell you things to come

II Peter 1:8 –For if these things are yours and abound, you will be neither barren nor unfruitful in the knowledge (epignosis) of our Lord Jesus Christ. (See verses 5-7)

II Corinthians 2:14 –Now thanks be to God who always leads us in triumph in Christ, and through us diffuses the fragrance of His knowledge (gnosis) in every place.

CHAPTER TEN

Rightly dividing the word of God.

The Bible is a mother lode of spiritual nuggets. It contains directions on how to know God, and receive eternal life. It defines good and evil, gives instructions for righteous living, and guidelines for the health and wellbeing of mankind. The correct way to discover, understand, and apply these nuggets is seek revelation from the Holy Spirit while reading the scriptures.

To rightly divide the word of truth simple means to accurately interpret and teach the scriptures as God intended them. The bible is written for the general benefit of all people groups. However, many of its passages are informative rather than directive for the Christian. Some scriptures are meant specifically for the Jews. Other passages are intended only for Christians. It is crucial for the bible student to rightly discern these differences.

Many Christians have been needlessly put in bondage to the law by doctrines that fail to separate the Old Covenant laws from the New Covenant of grace. The cross frees the believer from the law by the application of God's grace. The conditions of the Old Covenant should never be placed upon Christians.

Jesus fulfilled all the requirements of the Old Covenant laws and provided a New Covenant of grace for believers (Romans 6:14) Rightly dividing the covenants is critical to rightly applying the truths of the bible. The life and teachings of Jesus are powerful guides to understanding the meaning of many scriptures.

- Romans 8:3-4 – For what the law could not do in that it was weak through the flesh, God did by sending His own Son in the likeness of sinful flesh, on account of sin: He condemned sin in the flesh. (4) that the righteous requirements of the law might be fulfilled in us who do not walk according to the flesh but according to the Spirit.
- Romans 6:14 –For sin shall not have dominion over you, for you are not under law but under grace.

The misunderstanding of the difference of these two covenants has led to the development of doctrines that have confused the Christian community. It has caused dominations and individuals to mistakenly embrace beliefs that are contrary to God's true intent of the scriptures. The Old Covenant of the law only applied to the descendants of Abraham. The New Covenant includes all who believe in Jesus as the Son of God.

The scriptures themselves direct us to seek earnestly the true meaning and application of truths contained in them.

- II Timothy 2:15 – Be diligent to present yourself approved to God, a worker who does not need to be ashamed, rightly dividing the word of truth.
- II Timothy 3:16 –All scripture is given by inspiration of God, and is profitable for doctrine, for reproof, for correction, for instruction in righteousness.
- All scripture is profitable for the purpose it was given but not all scriptures apply to Christians.

Understanding what Jesus' death on the cross accomplished is vital to interpreting many scriptures. It is an important factor in determining whether or not a scripture applies to the Christian. The cross is the dividing line between the conditions and requirements of the Old and New Covenants.

Rightly interpreting scripture is vital to understanding its application to the believer. Scriptures can be examined by a few simple rules to determine those that pertain to Christians and those that do not. All scripture is given by inspiration of God, that is true, but not all scripture is directive to those under the New Covenant. That is not to say that it is not valuable to the Christian for all scripture was given by God for a purpose.

The following questions will help to determine if a scripture is instruction for the Christian.

- Did the intent of the scripture terminate at the cross?
- Did the intent of the scripture change at the cross?
- Did the principle of the scripture remain the same on the New Covenant side of the cross?

Examples:

1. Blood sacrifice <u>terminated</u> at the cross because Jesus was the final sacrifice for sin (Hebrews 10:1-14).
2. The Old Covenant Sabbath rest <u>changed</u> at the cross from being a physical day of rest to becoming a spiritual rest in the finished work of Jesus (Hebrews 4:4-11).
3. Scriptures that retain their principle under the New Covenant.

    - <u>Proverbs 4:23</u> – Keep your heart with all diligence for out of it spring the issues of life.
    - <u>Matthew 4:4</u> – But He answered and said, "It is written, "Man shall not live by bread alone, but by every word that proceeds from the mouth of God."
    - <u>Luke 15:11-32</u> – Story of the prodigal son

These are just a few examples because there are many truths in the Old Testament that are still valuable to the Christian. Christians are wise to use them as guidelines for their lives.

The following approach may also provide additional help to determine the proper meaning or application of passages of scripture from both the Old Testament and New Testament.

Regarding God:

- What is He saying: What does He mean?
- Who does what He is saying apply to: An individual, group, or everyone?
- Why is He saying it: What is His purpose?
- What is the context of what He is saying?

Regarding a particular scripture:

- Who was it written to? Is it directed to an individual, a specific group, or can it be applied to everyone?
- How does it relate to the passages that come before and after it?
- How does it relate to other scriptures regarding the same topic?
- What is the verse saying? What is its true meaning in its context? It is important to determine what God intended the scripture to mean.
- Does the scripture require the Christian to accomplish something that is a prerequisite to God loving or forgiving him?

EXAMPLE:

1. Matthew 6:14 –15 – "For if you forgive men their trespasses, your heavenly Father will also forgive you."

(15) "But if you do not forgive men their trespasses, neither will your Father forgive your trespasses.

This passage is obviously under the Old Covenant law. The death of Jesus on the cross secured forgiveness for all sin without conditions. It is very important that we confess our sins to God and to others. However, the forgiveness for sin is guaranteed by Jesus' sacrificial death, not by anything we can do. God's forgiveness does not depend upon our forgiving others. The thief on the cross was forgiven although he never asked for it.

2. I John 1:9 – If we confess our sins, He is faithful and just to forgive us our sins and to cleanse us from all unrighteousness.

This verse taken in the context of John's writings is apparent that he is giving directions on how to maintain a person's walk in the light with the Lord. Confessing sin is agreeing with God regarding good and evil. It maintains an open relationship with Him. However, to say that unless we confess our sins they will not be forgiven invalidates the purpose of Jesus' death on the cross.

- This verse begins with a condition "if". Meaning if we confess our sins He will forgive us. It assumes that if we do not confess He will not forgive us. If this interpretation is applied to the Christian it poses many problems.
- First, it implies that in order to confess all sins the person must be able to recall every sins, otherwise he could never be forgiven of those sins.
- Second, it indicates that a person's sins make him unrighteous; otherwise there would be no need for the cleansing. This would mean one is unrighteous until they confess their sins. Then they become unrighteous again as soon as they sin again. Therefore, righteous could only be a temporary state between a person's confession and his next sin. This would imply that a person's performance dictates his righteousness. The scriptures do not validate this position.
    - <u>II Corinthians 5:21</u> – for He made Him who knew no sin to be sin for us, that we might become the <u>righteousness of God in Him.</u>
    - <u>I Corinthians 1:30</u> – But of Him you are in Christ Jesus, who became for us wisdom from God- and <u>righteousness</u> and sanctification and redemption
    - <u>Romans 5:17</u> – For if by the one man's offense death reigned through the one, much more those who receive abundance of grace and of the <u>gift of righteousness</u> will reign in life through the One, Jesus Christ.
- How can we be the righteousness of God and unrighteous at the same time?
- If God does not remember our sins and He does not hold sin against us why would He still require us to confess them in order to be forgiven?

- Our forgiveness is based upon the death of Jesus on the cross not our confession.

  However, we must be extremely careful not to devalue the importance of confessing the sin in our life. It is the means of walking in the light with Him. We confess because we agree with God about the wrongs we commit.

To rightly divide the word and obtain the truths contained in the scriptures we much search both Old and New Testaments for those life principles that pertain to us as Christians and apply them in our lives as the guidelines for our Christian walk.

CHAPTER ELEVEN

Hearing God is essential to life.

The single most important thing that a person can do during his lifetime is to believe in Jesus Christ. It is his belief in Jesus that secures his place in eternity. It also gives him access to all the grace benefits of God.

Jesus alone is the source of eternal life. He is the means to having a successful, happy, contented, prosperous, healthy, and sin free life.

The second most important thing is to learn to listen to God. Reading the bible is not the same as listening to God. It is important to read and study the Bible, but it is no substitute for listening to Him. God may want to talk to you about something that is not in the Bible. If the Holy Spirit does not give us revelation of what we are reading it is of little benefit to us. Many Christians confess they do not hear God, or seek His guidance on life matters.

It is crucial for Christians to set aside a regular time to listen to God. To seek God's guidance in making decisions concerning the issues and wellbeing of their lives. People throughout the bible heard God and received specific guidance from Him. Christians have God's Spirit in them and the ability to hear His guidance on every aspect of their lives.

Jesus stressed the importance of listening to God in the following scripture:

- Man shall not live by bread alone but by every word that proceeds from the mouth of God (Matt. 4:4).
- The Greek for "word" here is "Rhema" which means a specific personal word from God.

- o God words are spirit and life. What He speaks to us will always be relevant to our individual needs (John 6:63).
- o Hearing God is simple as hearing others when we develop good listening habits with Him?
- o Hearing God does not depend upon our ability to hear Him but on His ability to communicate to those who wish His guidance.

The following are some hindrances to hearing God.

- Failing to set aside some time in our day to spend talking and listening to Him.
- Allowing obstacles such as the phone, others, chores, disruptive thoughts, and other worldly things to distract us when spending time with Him.
- Using a busy or full schedule as a reason for not spending time with Him.
- Not recognizing His voice, the way He speaks to you personally
- The devil does not want you to hear God and will attempt all manner of distractions to interrupt your time with God.
- Our flesh is not saved and acts like an unruly spoiled child. The flesh does not like to submit to the things of God and will resist listening to Him and doing things His way.
- Our minds have not been renewed completely so we still have beliefs and learned behavior that must be changed in order for us to comprehend the things of God

How does a person discern if it is the devil speaking? He speaks through our thoughts. He will normally speak in the first person to make you think they are your thoughts. i.e., "I hate them for ________". His thoughts will be negative, appeal to the flesh, or contradict biblical principles. Any thought that contradicts the righteous character of God or violates His Word comes from the devil or the flesh.

God may speak through our mind or spirit. His thoughts will always align with His written word. They will be constructive and encouraging. They will provide guidance and comfort as needed, and never condemn or criticize. We may also receive impressions from God through our human spirit.

It is difficult to discern the source of some thoughts. We may have thoughts that scriptures do not provide us with clear guidelines; thoughts that do not appear to be good or evil. This is where hearing God surpasses readings the bible. We can ask Him to enlighten us on these thoughts. When we learn listen to God and live by the things He shares we develop the mind of Christ.

Philippians 2:5 – Let this mind be in you which was also in Christ Jesus.

I Corinthians 2:16 – For "who has known the mind of the Lord that he may instruct Him?" But we have the mind of Christ.

To hear God we must actively practice listening to Him. We seek His input on events and issues of our life and apply what He tells us. His desire is that we hear Him. It pleases Him when we seek His advice. He is constantly communicating to us we just need to develop a hearing ear.

CHAPTER TWELVE

The Favor of God

One of the most amazing verses in the Bible is recorded in Luke 2:52. It is difficult for the human mind to understand how God who inhabits the universe could confine Himself to the human body. How He could restrict Himself to the process of physical growth. It is beyond human explanation how God who knows all things could restrict His knowledge and wisdom to the process of physical and mental maturity. All these challenge the mind, but how the Son of God had to grow in favor with the Father is beyond comprehension.

Luke 2:52 – And Jesus increased in wisdom and stature, and in favor with God and men

Through each stage of His life Jesus must have exhibited exemplary traits that caused Him to have favor with His family and others. His lack of sin and deep spiritual knowledge set Him apart from His peers. His first interaction with religious leaders was not typical for a twelve year old. As an adult, Jesus drew great crowds amazed by His compassion, teaching, and actions. They were filled with awe and wonder as they heard him teach and witnessed Him perform miracles. He attained favor with most of the ordinary people by addressing their needs with love and kindness.

Luke 2:40-50 gives us a glimpse of Jesus' early life. Luke states that as Jesus grew he became strong in spirit, was filled with wisdom, and the grace of God was upon Him. This is a remarkable testimony of one who had not yet reached His teens. As a pre-teen His total commitment to God,

His Father, was already established. It is evident that His earthly parents taught and guided Him through the formative years of His life.

They certainly helped to establish His identity by constantly reminding Him of the events surrounding His birth, and stressing God was His Father. They also must have taught Him the scriptures and provided Him with spiritual guidance.

Parents are critical in helping their children mature into the person that God designed them to become. Children in their formative years are very vulnerable to the actions, attitudes and words of adults, especially their parents. We can assume that Jesus' parents were good role models.

I understand why Jesus, as God, would restrict Himself to the vulnerability of human growth stages. This allowed Him to identify with us concerning the specific issues associated with each stage. I also have no difficulty believing that Jesus grew in favor with people. Consider the following:

- He certainly would have been a joy and a blessing to His parents. Each stage of His life would be a testimony of His uniqueness. He would have grown in their favor.
- The widow of Nain was grieving without hope. She had already lost her husband, and now she was on her way to bury her only son. Jesus stops the funeral procession, comforts her, and restores her son to life. We can only imagine the depth of gratitude that flooded the heart of this mother at the recovery of her son. We can say with full assurance that in her eyes Jesus surely grew in her favor. Her son was also rescued from death and given a second chance at life. She represents the many whose hopes have been restored_by the miraculous intervention of Jesus. Her son represents the many that have escaped death experiences (Luke 7:11-17).
- The demon possessed man of Gadara. He was tormented day and night, living without hope. He wandered in the graveyard among the dead without friend or family to help him. His life completely controlled by evil forces with no hope of recovery. This is his state when Jesus comes by divine appointment to his rescue. He casts out the demons and provides the man with clothes. The man's

sanity is restored and he once again has purpose in life. He returns to his family and friends praising Jesus. It is obvious from his response that Jesus grew in his favor. This man represents those who are desperately lost, driven by forces they can not control, whose only hope is Jesus (Mark 5:1-20).

- The woman suffering with a blood issue for twelve years. She has spent all her money on doctors without getting any relief. She has nearly given up hope when she hears about Jesus' compassion to heal people. She believes if she can just get close enough to Him to touch His clothing she will be healed. She did, and she was. When she realized that she no longer was burdened with her problem Jesus certainly grew in favor with her. She represents those with incurable diseases and unfixable problems that only the righteous power of a loving Savior can remedy. (Mark 5:25-34).
- The man was born blind. He had suffered the anguish of blindness every day for forty years. He had never experienced the beauty of a sunset, blue sky, blooming flowers, or any of the things that so many take for granted. He had surely been hurt by remarks he had overheard. Jesus' own disciples wanted to attribute the cause of his blindness to sin. Jesus gave him sight and he was introduced to a whole new world of wonder and awe. I imagine that with each new wonder Jesus grew in the favor of this man. He represents the millions who are spiritually blind that Jesus wishes to introduce to a whole new world. (John 9:1-41).
- The woman at the well. She had experienced rejection, ridicule, and shame met Jesus at a well. She had suffered through five failed marriages and was living in sin. Jesus introduces Himself as the Messiah and offers her eternal life. She is filled with hope and joy. Many men in her village were saved because of her testimony. Her encounter with Jesus surely caused Him to grow in favor with her. She represents the many who are suffering because of failed relationships, rejection, and guilt. (John 4:4-26).

It is easy to understand how Jesus grew in favor with all those in the bible that were blessed by Him. It is also easy to believe that Jesus has grown in favor with thousands through the centuries whose lives have been changed by Him. If your story was known it could also be included here.

What amazes me is how He, the Son of God, could increase in the favor of the Father who has always loved Him. They are inseparable. My finite mind must probe for a greater revelation that I can grasp.

Consider that before the beginning of creation Jesus was in complete union with the Father and the Holy Spirit as part of the Trinity. He took part in the divine plans for the redemption of man all prior to creation. He was slain before the foundation of the world for the sake of mankind so that men could be reconciled to God. Before He had healed any sick or performed any miracles the Father said at His water baptism that He was well pleased with His Son (Matthew 3:17). Again, on the Mount of Transfiguration the Father affirms that He was well pleased with His beloved Son (Matthew 17:5). So why, and how could Jesus grow in favor with the One who loved Him without measure? It should be understood here that the operative word is "favor" and not love, because the love of God for His Son has always been without measure.

I have concluded that the answer lies within the restrictions Jesus placed upon Himself as a human. Individuals must mature spiritually as well as physically through different stages before they are entrusted with greater responsibilities and enjoy more favor by assuming these responsibilities. In a similar manner there are favors of God that are only released as we mature enough to rightly appreciate and employ them. A father does not show favor to a ten year old by allowing him the use of the family automobile. Neither does God entrust spiritual favor to one who lacks the maturity to assume its responsibility.

More favor is granted to those whose maturity assures there will be no misuse of the favor. Jesus was restricted to the limitations of each stage of growth the same as other humans. The favors of these stages were also restricted until He reached the maturity to assume the responsibilities of the favor.

How can a person position himself to receive more favor from God? He can start by looking into the life of Jesus. On several occasions Jesus stated that He only did what the Father told Him to do or what He saw the Father doing. His total focus was on the will of the Father in every occasion of His life. Jesus' life is a demonstration of how we are to live.

The more we structure our lives after His example the more favor we will receive from God.

Jesus reveals His secret, or perhaps a better word would be His heart's attitude in Matthew 4:4. He emphatically declares that man must live by every word that proceeds from the mouth of God. For one to live by what God says that person must actively listen to God. Listening to God is a matter of life. Whatever God says to an individual will be something that will enrich his life, address his personal needs, and provide guidance.

There are examples in the Old and New Testaments of how a person can position himself to hear God. While in the wilderness Moses set up a "Tent of Meeting" outside the camp. Its purpose was to provide individuals with a secluded place to meet with God. It was outside the camp to avoid distractions. It was here Moses talked with God about current matters pertaining to their wilderness journey. Joshua also met with God in the tent. Every Israelite had the opportunity to meet with God in the tent. (Exodus 33:7-11).

In the New Testament Jesus provides us with a similar model. He instructs us to have a private place away from distractions where we can listen and talk to God. (Matthew 6:6). This time is often referred to as a quiet time with God. It is during these times a person learns to distinguish God's voice. As he listens he gains confidence in his ability to hear God on matters of interest.

More favor is granted as we grow spiritually. Spiritual maturity is the process of acquiring biblical knowledge and applying it in our lives. We change our paradigms to align with the truths we discover through bible study and time with God. The Holy Spirit tutors us through the stages of maturing. He uses the bible as our textbook. He provides us with the grace to adjust our lives to the spiritual principles of the Kingdom of God.

New Testament epistles were written specially for the purpose of guiding believers in adopting the ways of God. The Apostle Peter's second epistle contains such important guidelines.

- II Peter 1:5-9 - But also for this very reason, giving all diligence, add to your faith virtue, to virtue knowledge, (6) to knowledge self-control, to self-control perseverance, to perseverance godliness, (7) to godliness brotherly kindness, and to brotherly kindness love.

> (8) For if these things are yours and abound, you will be neither barren nor unfruitful in the knowledge of our Lord Jesus Christ. (9) For he who lacks these things is shortsighted, even to blindness, and has forgotten that he was cleansed from his old sins.

Throughout the day Christians are tempted with thoughts, situations, and circumstances of the world, flesh and devil. We must choose to respond accordingly. Peter identifies some of these temptations and provides guidance on how to respond. These verses are guideposts for maturing as we apply them in our daily encounters.

The following attributes are essential in the process of spiritual maturity. When we are challenged in these areas and respond biblically we are strengthened in spirit.

- <u>faith</u> – A response of our spirit without empirical evidence. We face faith challenges throughout our day.
- <u>Virtue</u> – Moral excellence. Purity of manner. Responding with virtue when we are tempted to act or think in an immoral manner.
- <u>Knowledge</u> – Acquiring biblical truth. (2 Peter 3:18).
- <u>Self-control</u> – Exercising restraint when tempted to respond in the flesh.
- <u>Perseverance</u> – Developing the mindset to overcome obstacles that hinder our Christian walk.
- <u>Godliness</u> - The pious mindset that dictate our thoughts and actions
- <u>Brotherly Kindness</u> – Having a benevolent attitude toward others, especially Christians.
- <u>Love</u> – Expressing unconditional benevolence under all circumstances.

Things that hinder favor with God.

A. Being offended at God.

<u>Believing that God failed to respond as expected has caused many to be offended. If we believe God is somehow</u>

negligent in His responsibilities toward us we become angry and reject Him.

There are many things concerning God that we may not understand. When unanswered questions arise we must direct our attention to the cross and the love that motivated God to send His Son in our place. When we do not understand we know His actions toward us are always motivated by His unconditional love for us. If we must have all our questions answered before we can trust God we will miss out on many acts of His favor.

It is okay to admit we don't understand many things about God, and why certain things happen. We do know that God is always good. He has proven His love for us by offering eternal salvation through His Son. The bible declares all His promises to us are affirmed (II Corinthians 1:20)

B. Becoming dull of hearing

Hebrews 5:11 – of whom we have much to say, and hard to explain, since you have become dull of hearing.

Matthew 13:15 – For the hearts of this people have grown dull. Their ears are hard of hearing, and their eyes they have closed, lest they should see with their eyes and hear with their ears, lest they should understand with their hearts and turn, so that I should heal them.

C. Distraction with things of the world.

Matthew 13:22 – Now he who received seed among the thorns is he who hears the word and the cares of this world and the deceitfulness of riches choke the word, and he becomes unfruitful.

D. Taking ungodly advice

Psalms 1:1 – Blessed is the man who walks not in the counsel of the ungodly.

E. A carnal lifestyle

I Corinthians 3:1-3 – And I, brethren, could not speak to you as to spiritual people but as to carnal, as to babes in

Christ. (2) I fed you with milk and not with solid food; for until now you were not able to receive it, and even now you are still not able; (3) for you are still carnal. For where there are envy, strife, and divisions among you, are you not carnal and behaving like mere men?

Romans 8: 5 – For those who live according to the flesh set their minds on the things of the flesh, but those who live according to the Spirit, the things of the Spirit.

- A carnal lifestyle is following the desires of the flesh and conforming to the world system.
- The basis of our faith is hearing the Holy Spirit. Carnality dulls our ability to hear. If we are unable to hear the Spirit we will live our lives based upon carnal decisions.
- A carnal person will respond negatively to the life situations in II Peter 1:5-8.

F. Rejecting the grace of God.

Galatians 5:1-4 – Stand fast therefore in the liberty by which Christ has made us free, and do not be entangled again with a yoke of bondage. (2) Indeed I, Paul, say to you that if you become circumcised, Christ will profit you nothing. (3) And I testify again to every man who becomes circumcise that he is a debtor to keep the whole law. (4) You have become estranged from Christ, you who attempt to be justified by law; you have fallen from grace.

- A person rejects the grace of God when he attempts to live by the laws of the Old Covenant. He trusts what he can do rather than what Jesus has done.

God loves us unconditionally and delights in blessing us with favor. Responsibility comes with favor. He wisely releases favor as we become mature enough to demonstrate it. The Holy Spirit prepares us to receive more of God's favor by tutoring us through our maturing process.

CHAPTER THIRTEEN

Examining predestination in the light of the gospel of grace.

The purpose of this Chapter is to provide biblical evidence that God does not willfully predestine people to hell without giving them a choice for redemption. He has in fact, done everything possible to keep them from going to hell. He expressed unconditional love for all mankind by sending His Son to die on a cruel cross for them. He reconciled the world to Himself and forgave all sin. Jesus' death for the redemption of men would have been a meaningless act if man's destiny was decided without a choice on his part.

This study affirms the sovereignty of God. It acknowledges that salvation is totally God's plan. It fosters the idea that the wisdom and plan of God is so great and magnificent that it reconciles any perceived differences between predestination and the choice of men.

Understanding the nature of God is critical to interpreting and applying the scriptures. It is also crucial in deveoping correct doctrines of His purpose for creating mankind. Distorted images of God has led some to view God as a Creator who arbitrarily creates some for Heaven and others for Hell. Most theologians agree that God is sovereign; that all men are born spiritually dead and have no desire or ability to seek God. They also agree that the redemption of man depends entirely upon the grace of God apart from anything man can accomplish. Therefore, God must reveal their lost condition, and provide them with faith to respond to His invitation of salvation. He extends His invitation to all mankind.

Most theologians agree with this view. However, others teach that mankind is totally depraved, and God is justified in allowing many to remain in this state while rescuing others. They say He chooses certain ones for salvation but does not choose others. God in His sovereignty predestines some to heaven and the remainder go to hell. He is justified in doing so because all fallen mankind deserves hell. The following is a summary of this belief:

The Reformed Faith has held to the existence of an eternal, divine decree which, antecedently to any difference or desert in men themselves separates the human race into two portions and ordains one to everlasting life and the other to everlasting death. So far as this decree relates to men, it designates the counsel of God concerning those who had a supremely favorable chance in Adam to earn salvation, but who lost that chance. As a result of the fall they are guilty and corrupted; their motives are wrong and they cannot work out their own salvation. They have forfeited all claim upon God's mercy, and might justly have been left to suffer the penalty of their disobedience as all of the fallen angels were left. But instead the elect members of this race are rescued from this state of guilt and sin and are brought into a state of blessedness and holiness. The non-elect are simply left in their previous state of ruin, and are condemned for their sins. They suffer no unmerited punishment, for God is dealing with them not merely as men but as sinners. (Loraine Boettner, The Reformed Doctrine of Predestination) This outlines the perimeters of predestination.

This doctrine embraces the belief that before the beginning of creation God predetermined the fate of all mankind. He chose to saved some and left the rest in their depraved state. He is justified in doing this since all are depraved. It is out of His love and mercy that He delivers some. This implies that God willfully creates a human race knowing that part of them are destined to be tormented in hell for eternity. But, He is a loving God because He allows some to be saved. The basis of His choices is his foreknowledge that Adam would sin and cause all mankind to be depraved.

The obvious question is how does this picture of God align with the Scriptures? The bible declares that God is love, merciful, forgiving, kind, and benevolent. This is the picture of God demonstrated by the life of Jesus, the exact image of God.

It is an irrefutable fact that God is sovereign and whatever He chooses to do is appropriate and just. It is also irrefutable that God must first approach man and enlighten him before the man can respond, and then only after God gives him faith. This is indeed an act of love that can only be attributed to God. Man does not have the power nor wisdom to save himself. Very few theologians would argue this biblical truth. The very willingness of God, as the scriptures validate, to extend salvation grace to all men should be evidence that He does not willfully predestine some to eternal punishment.

Any interpretation of the scriptures that depict God as willing to sentence a person to hell without giving that person a chance for heaven is a distorted image of God. It does not accurately depict the heart of the God who sent His beloved Son to prevent people from going to hell. Jesus portrayed a Father with a forgiving heart of mercy willing to save and heal all who would come to Him.

A cursory study of the scriptures and the life of Jesus will reveal the truth that God is a loving and compassionate God that does not wish any to perish. The bible states very clearly that Jesus died for the sins of all people, not just a certain number. It declares that the grace of God that brings salvation has appeared to all men teaching them to live soberly. It is not God's will that any should perish. He promises that anyone who believes in His Son will be saved. For God to say that it is not His will for any to perish and then predestine some to perish without a choice would be a contradiction both of His character and word.

Those who believe in limited attonement teach that Jesus shed His blood only for those chosen for heaven. However, there are many scriptures that clearly state He died for the sins of all mankind. It is through the shedding of Jesus' blood that God reconciled the world to Himself. He declares He no longer remembers sin. To teach that the blood of Jesus was shed only for those arbitrarily chosen by God diminishes the purpose of His death. It nullifies His love for all people, and ignores many scriptures that state the very opposite.

If a person starts with the premise that God predetermined before time the fate of all mankind then he must conclude that God made this choice apart from any and all other reasons. Nothing following this choice could change the outcome. If this were true there would be no valid reason for Jesus to come to earth. The decision of who was to be saved had already been made. His death on the cross would not have an effect upon the predestined choice of God. There could be no redemptive purpose for Jesus' death. To believe otherwise would be to acknowledge the death of Jesus did have an effect on who was to be saved. The belief that God had already preordained all who were to be saved would be an untenable position.

If such a doctirne were true it would be foolish to have churches or individuals to demonstrate the Christian life or preach the gospel (good news). It could not be good news knowing you may already be preselected for a destiny of which you have no choice. A person's destiny would not be effected by what he believes about Jesus nor how righteously he lives but totally on a predetermined choice of God. It would have already been decided apart from anything he could do, good or evil.

Another belief regarding predestination should also be considered. The belief that it was necessary for Jesus to die for those chosen. Why? What would be the purpose if God had already made the decision in eternity past. It would be foolishness for Jesus to have to die for those that God had already predetermined would be saved. What would His death accomplish? They were already saved! Why would Jesus need to die for something that was already decided before hand? Why would God determine who was to be saved then design a plan that would include the death of the One He loved so that His choice would be justified?

Another consideration is if the choice of God was made prior to man being created it could have nothing to do with the depraved state of the person. The answer can not be the foreknowledge of God. (1) It would not be a matter of who God foreknew would respond and who would not since all would be depraved and unable to respond. The choice would be completely God's because mankind would have no control over his birth, depravity or choice of destiny. (2) Foreknowledge is man's word that attempts to describe having knowledge of an event before it happens. Actually, God does not exist on a timeline that includes past, present, and future. He exists always in the present now. (3) Certainly God is omniscient and knows all who will respond and be saved.

Those who believe in predestination teach that since we do not know who the elect are we must preach the gospel so the ones that are chosen can respond. Would this include non-elect, who think they are the elect, attempting to demonstrate something that they are not included in? If in fact, God has already made His choices why would there be a need for churches, missionaries, evangelists or teachers of the gospel? If a person must hear and respond to the gospel before he/she can be counted as one of the elect then it would be the individual's choice not the preselection of God that determined his salvation.

To say a person must respond to an invitation to accept Jesus as savior before he/she can be saved would seem to invalidate the predestination theory. If man's destiny is predetermined, the whole issue of praying for the lost is a futile exercise. If a person is not one of the elect any effort to persuade him to be saved would be useless. The other side of the coin would also be true, no amount of denying God, His existence or His love could prevent one of the elect from being saved. To deny this validates the teaching that indeed man does have a choice in where he is to spend eternity.

If a person must respond to the gospel then they have a choice. Then the preaching of the gospel makes good sense. If preaching the gospel allows men to respond to God's invitation to be saved, then the preaching of the gospel becomes very important in the plan of God. We can say that God has predestined all who believe in His Son will be saved. Knowing this motivates men and women to serve as missionaries to all the nations of the world.

The Holy Spirit calls evanglists to carry the good news to all people groups in an effort to reach the lost. God ordained churches to teach the truths of the bible; to equip their congregations to demonstrate and share the benefits of their new life in Christ. None of these would have a valid purpose if the destiny of all men were already predetermined by God.

God's grace offers salvation to all who will believe in His Son. Consider the following scriptures:

<u>II Peter 3:9</u> - The Lord is not slack concerning His promise, as some count slackness but is long suffering toward us, not willing that <u>any</u> should perish but <u>all</u> should come to repentance.

- There would be no need for the Lord to be long suffering if He has already predestined that a person is forever lost. What would be the purpose? Long suffering only makes sense if He is granting more time to individuals so that they can respond and be saved.

- "Not His will that any should perish but that ALL should come to repentance". The interpretative words for this verse are "any" and "all" If it is not His will that any should perish then it must be His desire that ALL should be saved. It can not be both ways. He can not have a will that chooses some to go to hell and at the same time have a will that He does not wish any should perish. If He alone has the power to save, and if He has already predetermined the fate of all, why would He say that it is not His will that any should perish? If He predetermines some to hell it would certainly be his will for some to perish. If it is not His will that any should perish and many do perish there must be a choice the individual can make to circumvent the will of God. The scriptural view of this verse would include John 3:16 and many others that correctly identify God as a loving, long suffering, merciful, kind and benevolent person who in His great love and mercy sent His Son to open the gate of salvation so whosoever will may come. He sent the Holy Spirit to enlighten men and draw them to God. He then furnishes them with the grace and faith to respond. Hallelujah!!!

Titus 2:11 - The grace of God that brings salvation has appeared to all men.

- Why would a God who has already predetermined who is to be saved and who is to remain lost still present people with the grace that enables them to be saved? Why present grace to those who have no capacity to respond?

I Timothy 2:3-4 - For this is good and acceptable in the sight of God our Savior, who desires all men to come to the knowledge of the truth.

- If God desires ALL men to come to the knowledge of the truth then they must have a choice. Jesus said, "I am the way, the truth, and the life. (John 14:6).

Ezekiel 18:23 - Do I have any pleasure at all that the wicked should die?
Ezekiel 18:32 - "For I have no pleasure in the death of one who dies....

- Is it possible that God who has no pleasure in the death of the wicked would knowing destine them to such a place as hell? I think not.

Isaiah 53: 4-6 – Surely He has borne our griefs and carried our sorrows; Yet we esteemed Him stricken, smitten by God, and afflicted. (5) But He was wounded for our transgressions, He was burised for our iniquities; The chastisement for our peace was upon Him, and by His stripes we are healed. (6) All we like sheep have gone astray; we have turned, every one, to his own way; And the Lord has laid on Him the iniquity of us all.

I Peter 2:24 – who Himself bore our sins in His own body on the tree, that we, having died to sins, might live for righteousness – by whose stripes you were healed.

Hebrews 10:12 - But this man, after He had offered one sacrifice for sins forever, sat down at the right hand of God.

Hebrews 10: 17 - Then He adds, "their sins and lawless deeds I will remember no more

Hebrews 10:18 - Now where there is remission of these, there is no longer an offering for sin".

John 1:29 - The next day John saw Jesus coming toward him, and said, "Behold! The Lamb of God who takes away the sin of the world.

I John 2:2 - And He Himself is the propitiation for our sins, AND NOT FOR OURS ONLY BUT ALSO FOR THE WHOLE WORLD.

II Corinthians 5:14-15 – For the love of Christ compels us, because we judge thus: that if One died for all, then all died; (15) and He died for all, that those who live should live no longer for themselves, but for Him who died for them and rose again.

- There is no ambiguity in these verses. Jesus died for all the sins of the world not just a chosen number. The death of Jesus on the cross was God's means of dealing with the depravity of mankind.

II Corinthians 5:18 - Now all things are of God who has reconciled us to Himself through Jesus Christ, and has given us the ministry of reconciliation.

- The question arises here that if God has already chosen the elect what is the purpose of a ministry of reconciliation? He clearly states what this ministry is in verse 19

II Corinthians 5:19 - that is, that God was in Christ reconciling the WORLD to Himself, not imputing their trespasses to them, and has committed to us the word of reconciliation.

- Several truths emerge here. (1) That Jesus' death on the cross reconciled the lost world to Himself. We base our salvation on the fact that what Jesus came to do, He completed. If He only died for the elect why would God say that the purpose for His Son coming was to make things right between God and the lost world? Jesus did all that was necessary for every person to be able to come to God. God left no walls erected between Him and lost mankind. This does not mean as some teach, that all men are going to heaven. There still remains the response of the individual to the invitation to believe in Jesus. (2) If God is not imputing sin to the lost then He would be unjust to send individuals to hell because of their depraved condition.
- Men who have not been born again spiritually are controlled by their sinful carnal nature. They can be depraved, corrupt, perverted, immoral and deviant which leads to all manner of sins. This scripture states that all the trespasses of man are not imputed or charged to them. If they have been forgiven by God are they still considered depraved by the God who forgave them of the sins?

John 1:12 - But as many as received Him, to them He gave the right to become children of God, to those who believe in His name.

- He came to His own people and they rejected Him but for those who did believe He made children of God. This does not say as many as were elected.

John 3:16 – For God so loved the world that He gave His only begotten Son, that whoever believes in Him should not perish but have everlasting life.

- This famous scripture has given comfort to men through the years. It emphatically states that God loved the people of the world in their lost condition so strongly that He willingly sacrificed His beloved Son so they could have eternal life and not perish. God has preordained and predestined that all who believe in His Son would not perish.

John 5:24 - Most assuredly, I say to you, "he who hears My word and believes in Him who sent Me has everlasting life, and shall not come into judgment, but has passed from death into life.

- Jesus gives the asssurance that any person who believes what He taught about God would receive everlasting life. It states the person has a choice, and adds credence to the mandate to take the gospel into all the world.

Romans 10:13 - For whoever calls on the name of The Lord shall be saved.

Acts 2:21 - And it shall come to pass that whoever calls on the name of The Lord shall be saved.

- Regardless of whoever calls on the name of The Lord they shall be saved. There is a choice involved and where there is a choice how could it be predetermined?

The bible declares the nature of God is love. He is also a God of grace. All of His actions toward mankind are motivated by His love and grace. He created a species of human beings to share His love, which He extends through grace. He invites every human being to share an eternal relationship with Him. Every individual can come just as he is because the invitation includes everything necessary for responding. This invitation is sealed in blood and is delivered personally by Jesus, the Son of God, with "RSVP". The individual must believe the messenger and the message.

The bible also states that Jesus' death on the cross made it possible for every person to receive an invitation. God has predestined that anyone who believes in Jesus Christ will be accepted.

Jesus' life, ministry, and teachings depict accurately the true nature of God the Father. Any image that reveals Him as a heartless god who creates beings for an eternity in hell is completely false. Any interpretation of the scriptures that suggest God is like that should be questioned.

The heart of the gospel of grace centers around the truth that God's love for the lost was the compelling factor that sent Jesus to die in their place so they would not perish. It is the work of the Holy Spirit alone that leads a person to understand his need to be saved. The Spirit also provides the person with faith to receive eternal life.

God has given Christians a mandate to take the message of reconciliation to the lost world. He calls His church to model the attributes of His kingdom, and teach converts the tenets of the gospel. It is an entangled web of misinterpretations of a myriad of scriptures that teach God does not offer His love and salvation to all mankind.

CHAPTER FOURTEEN

Tithing or Grace giving

This chapter provides a template that introduces the Christian to relational giving rather than regulation giving. By relational giving I mean giving out of our relationship with God. Under His guidance we give our time, money, and resources to help those in our sphere of influence. The topic of whether a Christian is required by the scriptures to tithe has been the subject of an ongoing debate. It is my intention to present biblical evidence that there is a higher reason for giving, than tithing. Giving that provides a holistic approach to benevolence. The Christian's motive for giving is their love for God and others. It is also my desire that those who feel the crunch of having to tithe at the expense of other needs will understand God never intended it to be so.

The Bible is printed into two major divisions, the Old and New Testaments. These divisions represent two major covenants with completely different terms. The Christian must understand these differences to accurately form his doctrinal beliefs. He can not attach the terms of the Old Covenant to the New Covenant. To do so will cause confusion and bondage to the individual. Is this what we have done with tithing?

If Christians are taught that they must tithe it should be supported by sound biblical proof. This is lacking in many pulpits today. Some reasons given why Christians should tithe are: (1) To acknowledge they understand everything they have is the result of God's generosity, (2) So that God will bless them i.e. "give and it shall be given unto you", (3) To show God they are grateful for all He has provided, (4) To keep from robbing God, (5) It is a requirement established by God. The troubling questions associated with each of these will be addressed later in this study.

First, let's look how the money collected for the tithe is used and compare to its Old Testament use. It is used to pay the salary and necessities of the pastor. It provides the finances for church programs, ministries, and the necessary upkeep of the church properties. Therefore, it is understandable why collecting the tithe is so important to church leadership. Mostly, these are valid needs for the church to function as a biblical influence in its sphere of responsibility. The question is whether or not God has ordered the tithe as the method of meeting these needs. Some may consider the tithe to be a tax that the church places on a person once they become a Christian. Under the law the tithe was given to the priests and Levites with clear instructions from God as to how it was dispersed. There was no guessing how God wanted it used.

The following situations are presented to give a better understanding of how individuals are affected when told they must tithe.

Consider situations similar to this. A widow lives off her social security check of $1300.00 each month. Her tithe is $130.00 each month. Her living expenses include her rent of $500.00, groceries $200.00, utilities, insurances, and miscellaneous total $300.00 and medicine and medical expenses are $200.00 for a total of $1200.00. She has $100.00 left to spend on unbudgeted items. She feels guilt for being unable to tithe and believes she forfeits the benefits promised from the pulpit. She has been told if she did not tithe she was robbing God, and did not trust Him. Does her inability to tithe forfeit God's blessings for her? Does this reveal to God that she fails to realize that everything she has comes from Him? Does this prove to God that she is not grateful for her monthly income? Should she do without her basic needs in order not to rob God? All these are valid questions when confronting situations where individuals can not tithe. It is obvious that the requirement to tithe can not be met in all instances. Certainly a loving Father would not withhold good nor think less of the person because they are unable to tithe.

Situation two: John is a faithful tithing Christian. He has a good job and his salary allows him to provide for the needs of his family and to put $1000.00 into savings each month. However, his wife requires emergency surgery and his medical bills are in the thousands. He depletes his savings account and borrows additional money in order to pay his bills. His monthly credit bill is nearly the same amount as his tithe. He has been assured from the pulpit that if he tithes God will take care of all his needs. He is forced to make an emotional decision between his needs and what he has been taught is his Christian responsibility.

Many Christians reveal they have tithed at the expense of meeting their personal responsibilities and have been sorely disappointed when God did not provide. Why? Where is this directive found in New Testament writings? Does God test a person's faith by expecting him to tithe rather than pay his bills? Christians are taught to be responsible citizens. When they have the resources to meet their obligations they should do so.

Circumstances and the lack of resources make it impossible for many to tithe. Every church has members that are unable to tithe for various reasons. They are placed under a cloud of guilt by messages declaring they must tithe. Christians in third world countries seldom have enough food for their families, and some must walk several miles to get safe drinking water. Only a person with a distorted understanding of God would believe that He would hold these accountable to tithe.

The first recorded instance of tithing is in Genesis Chapter fourteen. Abraham's nephew Lot and his family have been taken captive by hostile kings. Abraham takes his servants and defeats the hostile kings and rescues Lot and his family. He recovers the spoils of war taken by the kings. When he returns from his victory he is greeted by Melchizedek. Melchizedek served Abraham bread and wine and blessed him because of his association with God most high. He also blessed God for giving him the victory over his enemies. Abraham responded out of a heart of genuine gratitude by giving a tenth of the spoils to Melchizedek.

What is known about Melchizedek? He was a priest of the Most High God, King of Salem, King of righteousness, and King of peace. He had no earthly father or mother. There was not a time when his life began and no time for it to end. He was made like the Son of God. (See also Daniel 3:25). The only person who fulfills all these characteristics is the Lord Jesus. Melchizedek must have possessed divine knowledge about Abraham's battle to know when and where to meet him when he returned. King of Salem means king of peace. However, it is not known if Salem was his title or a physical place over which he ruled. It is reasonable to think that if it was a physical location, Abraham would have made an effort to contact him again. It is not known what Melchizedek did with the tithes of gold, silver, livestock, and other miscellaneous items. There is no record of Melchizedek ever appearing again as a priest.

What do the scriptures reveal about Abraham? He had a personal relationship with God. God appeared to him on several occasions before and after his meeting with Melchizedek. He worshipped God and wherever he went, he built altars on which he probably offered sacrifices to God. God made a covenant with him and promised to bless him and take care of him. Abraham's only response to God's covenant was to believe God. God counted Abraham's belief as righteousness. There were no conditions of this covenant that required Abraham to tithe. Melchizedek blessed him before he tithed, and not because he tithed.

The first recorded event of anyone giving to God is the story of Cain and Abel in Genesis chapter four where each brought an offering. If a tithe at been required by God certainly the first family would have known it, but instead of a tithe they brought an offering. There is no record of Adam doing either. Since there was no precedence for tithing from God it was Abraham's decision on how much he chose to give Melchizedek. He could have given it all, or whatever percentage he chose. Abraham's giving expressed his attitude of gratefulness. This is the heart attitude that motivates true grace giving. Abraham tithed out of his spoils of war. There is no biblical record that he ever tithed his personal wealth. Although he had many other encounters with God, there is no evidence that he ever tithed again. There is no record that Abraham's son, Isaac tithed; surely Abraham would have taught him to tithe if were a requirement.

There is no record that Jacob, his twelve sons, or any of Abraham's descendants tithed prior to the giving of the law. Genesis chapter twenty eight records Jacob promising God he would tithe if God met certain conditions. However, there is no record that Jacob ever followed through on that promise.

Some Christian leaders today use Abraham's tithe to Melchizedek as their basis for Christian tithing. They reason that since this was the first mention of tithing in the scriptures it set precedence because it superseded the giving of the law to Moses. However, using Abraham as the reason Christians should tithe is a poor example for the following reasons. First,

Abraham never tithed out of his personal wealth. Second, Abraham only tithed once. Third, Abraham evidently did not teach his son to tithe. Fourth, if Abraham's tithing is used as the precedence, his circumcision as a sign of righteousness and covenant must also be used the precedence. Abraham was also the first to participate in this rite. There is stronger evidence for circumcision because God directed Abraham regarding circumcision but there is no record of God directing him to tithe. However, Christians are not required to be circumcised because Abraham was, so why tithing?

There is a mountain of evidence that tithing was a requirement under the Old Covenant law. Moses was given clear instructions about who was to tithe, what they were to tithe, and the purpose of the tithe. There is no disputing this evidence. The law described precisely what the tithe was and how it was to be distributed.

However, this Old Covenant with all its requirements was made obsolete and terminated by the New Covenant. Jesus has fulfilled all the Old Covenant requirements for the Christian. Evidence that the Old Covenant is terminated is found in the following scriptures.

- Hebrews 8:6 "But now He has obtained a more excellent ministry, inasmuch as He is also Mediator of a better covenant, which was established on better promises.
- Hebrews 8:13 –"In that He says, "A new covenant", He has made the first obsolete. Now what is becoming obsolete and growing old is ready to vanish away.
- Matthew 5:17 "Do not think that I have come to destroy the Law or the Prophets. I did not come to destroy but to fulfill".
- Romans 10:4 –"For Christ is the end of the law for righteousness to everyone who believes".
- Romans 8:4 – that the righteous requirement of the law might be fulfilled in us who do not walk according to the flesh but according to the Spirit.
- It would seem reasonable to believe that if Jesus fulfilled the whole law it included tithing. Both Paul and James warn the Christian that if he wishes to keep one of the Old Testament laws

he is obligated to keep them all or if he breaks one he is guilty of breaking them all (Galatians 5:1-5, James 2:10).

The obvious omission of biblical references to tithing after the resurrection of Jesus should raise some doubts about it validity for the Christian. Paul, a devout and learned Pharisee was a guardian of the doctrines of the Old Covenant of Judaism. After his encounter with Jesus on the road to Damascus, Jesus told him that his ministry would be to the Gentiles. Following his conversion he was led by the Holy Spirit to spend three years in Arabia. There he received the revelation of the grace messages which he taught to the Gentile churches. He adamantly declares that he did not get his message from any person but his revelations came directly from God. He believed so strongly that the message of grace was true that he was willing to lay down his life in order to write and teach the grace gospel to the Gentiles.

Much of the theology and doctrines of the modern church are derived from Paul's writings. Paul was a good steward of the revelations that God gave him for the Gentile churches and taught with fervency the things the Holy Spirit had revealed to him. He wrote thirteen books that contain these revelations and never once mentions tithing.

- Galatians 1:11-18 – But I make known to you, brethren that the gospel which was preached by me is not according to man. (12) for I neither received it from man, nor was I taught it, but it came through the revelation of Jesus Christ (13) for you have heard of my former conduct in Judaism, how I persecuted the church of God beyond measure and tried to destroy it (14) And I advanced in Judaism beyond many of my contemporaries in my own nation, "being more exceedingly zealous for the traditions of my fathers. (15) But when it pleased God, who separated me from my mother's womb and called me through grace (16) to reveal His Son in me, that I might preach Him among the Gentiles, I did not immediately confer with flesh and blood. (17) nor did I go up to Jerusalem to those who were apostles before me; but I went to Arabia, and returned again to Damascus. (18) Then after three years I went up to Jerusalem to see Peter, and remained with him fifteen days.

- Ephesians 3:1-3 – For this reason I, Paul, the prisoner of Christ Jesus for you Gentiles- (2) if indeed you have heard of the dispensation of the grace of God which was given to me for you, (3) how that by revelation He made known to me the mystery (as I have briefly written already, (4) by which, when you read, you may understand my knowledge in the mystery of Christ)

John, the beloved apostle of Jesus, wrote five books of our bible and does not mention tithing. Peter wrote two books and does not mention tithing; Luke, who traveled with Paul, does not mention tithing in his record of the early church in the book of Acts. In Acts chapter fifteen there was a dispute regarding whether or not Gentiles were required to follow parts of the Old Covenant laws. The dispute was resolved by the Jerusalem elders, who sent a letter to the Gentile churches stating what was required of them. The letter closes with these two verses in Acts.

- Acts 15:27-28 – "For it seemed good to the Holy Spirit, and us, to lay upon you no greater burden than these necessary things; that you abstain from things offered to idols, from blood, from things strangled, and from sexual immorality. If you keep yourselves from these, you will do well.

The objective of the elders was to relieve Gentile churches from the burdens of the law. The obvious omission of tithing in the instructions to the Gentile churches is a clear indicator that tithing was not required of the Church. The elders state specifically they received their guidance from the Holy Spirit. If tithing was a requirement for New Testament Churches the Holy Spirit would have instructed some of the writers to include it in His directives for the Church. The absence of references to tithing as it relates to those under the New Covenant seems to be by divine intent.

Some who support tithing use Hebrews chapter seven where it states that Levi paid tithes. They reason since Levi was in Abraham's loins when he tithed to Melchizedek it counted as Levi tithing. Therefore Christians should also tithe because this event took place prior to the inception of the law. However, the overall theme of the book of Hebrews is the superiority of the priesthood of Jesus as compared to earthly high priests assigned under the law. The reference to tithing in chapter seven must be interpreted in this context.

Hebrews 7:4-9 – Now consider how great this man was, to whom even the patriarch Abraham gave a tenth of the spoils. (5) And indeed those who are of the sons of Levi, who receive the priesthood, have a commandment to receive tithes from the people according to the law, that is, from their brethren, though they have come from the loins of Abraham, (6) but he whose genealogy is not derived from them received tithes from Abraham and blessed him who had the promises. (7) Now beyond all contradiction the lesser is blessed by the better. (8) Here mortal men receive tithes, but there he receives them, of whom it is witnessed that he lives. (9) Even Levi, who receives tithes, paid tithes through Abraham, so to speak, (10) for he was still in the loins of his father when Melchizedek met him.

Hebrews 8:1-2 – Now this is the main point of the things we are saying; we have such a High Priest, who is seated at the right hand of the throne of the Majesty in the heavens, (2) a Minister of the sanctuary and of the true tabernacle which the Lord erected, and not man".

The clear message in these scriptures is that Jesus is a priest after the order of Melchizedek which is far superior to any priest of the Old Covenant. This comparison is illustrated by the reference to Levi who received tithes under the law, gave tithes to Melchizedek, being in the loins of Abraham. There is no clear directive that indicates Christians should tithe in these verses. It is mere conjecture to use these verses as proof text for tithing.

Most Christian leaders do not intend to place a financial burden on their congregations by teaching tithing. They sincerely have the best interest of there congregation in mind. By examining some of the reasons given for tithing we can apply those same reasons to grace giving. We can maintain the right attitude toward giving while avoiding those things that place us in bondage. Some reasons given for a Christian to tithe:

A. So that God will bless. The intent here is to position the Christian to receive more blessing from God by following the biblical principle found in Luke 6:38. This stresses reciprocal giving i.e., "give and it shall be given to you". To teach we must tithe for God to bless us is not biblical. God's blessings are not limited to how we give. This principle of grace giving in Luke includes all manner of things other than money. It applies regardless of what a person gives or the amount he gives. To teach otherwise indicates God only blesses those that tithe.

Luke 6:38 – Give, and it will be given to you: good measure, pressed down, shaken together, and running over will be put into your bosom. For with the same measure that you use, it will be measured back to you."

II Corinthians 8:12 – For if there is first a willing mind, it is accepted according to what one has, and not according to what he does not have. (2) It may cause a person to believe the bad things happen to them because they do not tithe. The principle of reciprocal giving is a valid one but unless tithing is taught as a voluntary act, it should not be used to solicit God's blessings.

B. To show God we realize that everything we have comes from His generosity. This is a great motive for generous giving in all facets of our lives. Christians realize that everything we have comes from God. That we are His stewards to give accordingly. We do not have to tithe every week to validate this.

C. To indicate to God we are grateful for all He has provided and done for us. Again this is a valid reason for one to give generously as God directs. How many times must a person tithe to prove this? There are numerous ways of expressing gratefulness to God other than giving money.

D. We rob God if we do not tithe. If God has not directed us to tithe, we can not be stealing. This indicates that God has a portion and the rest is ours, when in reality it all belongs to God. There are worse ways of robbing God than not tithing. How does this apply to those who can not tithe?

E. It is a biblical reqirement. The only biblical requirement for tithing was under the Old Covenant law and that only pertained to the nation of Israel. There is not a single verse in the bible after the resurrection of Jesus and the initiation of the New Covenant that requires the Christian to tithe.

Who is the recipient of the tithe and where is the designated place for the tithe to be received? Those that teach tithing say the tithe should be given to the local church where one attends because the church is the store house and designated place to worship God. This interpretation is extracted from the Old Testament. There God specifically designated a place where He would meet with His people and where they were to bring their tithes and worship Him. This place was the store house where the assigned priests received the tithes. However, in the New Testament all believers are priests, and their bodies are the temple where God abides. We can say that we are the priests of our temples. Through the finished work of Jesus God no longer resides in temples, tabernacles, or church buildings. Instead, He makes the body of believers His temple. His presence is with us always. Therefore we can worship Him at any time regardless of the place. Certainly we can say that God meets with His people wherever they gather in church buildings to corporately worship Him. However, Since God indwells believers when they leave the church building, God's presence also leaves. All believers are priests, are priests required to tithe?

There is no biblical evidence that Gentile church leaders such as Paul, Timothy, and Titus ever received tithes in the churches they served. There is much evidence that they taught those in their churches to give generously. Paul was often helped in his ministry by the support he received from individuals and churches.

Since we are His priests God may direct us to give our money or resources to meet or support needs outside the church. Where tithing is taught as a requirement, there are many unanswered questions that have no biblical answers.

Another consideration is believers are the church. The church is the Bride of Christ, not the Lord Himself. Does this mean that the Bride must tithe what the Groom has given her? It would be similar to a husband and wife having a joint bank account. Where he requires her to withdraw a tenth every week and give it to him to prove she really loves him and knows he is the bread winner.

In Romans chapter eight we are declared to be heirs and joint heirs with Christ. Does God require us to take what He says is ours jointly and give it back to Him for any of the purposes listed above. When did the tithe change to include just money?

Most of those who preach tithing would have difficulty with these verses:

- Deuteronomy 14:23-26 – And you shall eat before the Lord your God, in the place where He chooses to make His name abide, the tithe of your grain and your new wine and your oil, of the firstborn of your herds and your flocks, that you may learn to fear the Lord your God always. But if the journey is too long for you, so that you are not able to carry the tithe, or if the place where the Lord your God chooses to put His name is too far from you, when the Lord your God has blessed you, then you shall exchange it for money, take the money in your hand, and go to the place which the Lord your God chooses. And you shall spend that money for whatever your heart desires: for oxen or sheep, for wine or similar drink, for whatever your heart desires; you shall eat there before the Lord your God, and you shall rejoice, you and your household.

The following is a review of a few of the problems associated with tithing. First, if tithing is a requirement to not tithe would be a sin. This places a burden of guilt on many that can not tithe. Secondly, is money the only thing a person must tithe? Thirdly, must the tithe be paid at the expense of meeting other obligations or needs? Fourthly, is God displeased with those who do not tithe? Fifthly, Does God withhold His blessings from those who do not tithe? Sixth, if a person does not tithe does he forfeit God's protection from disasters and sickness? Seventh, if one gives a portion of his tithe to meet the need of another instead of giving it to the church is it a sin? Eighth, how many times must a person tithe to prove to God that he understands that all blessings are from Him? Ninth, if tithing is actually a part of the Old Covenant and a person tithes does that require the person to keep all of the Old Covenant Laws? (Galatians 5:3, James

2:10) These are just some of the problems associated with tithing that are never addressed from the pulpit.

The principle of grace giving as presented by Jesus far outweighs tithing, and more accurately portrays the heart of a loving and giving God. There are no laws under the New Covenant. The only requirement for gaining access to all the benefits of the New Covenant is to believe in Jesus Christ, as the Son of God. Under the New Covenant, the Christian is provided everything that pertains to life and godliness.

When grace giving is rightly taught there will always be finances to provide for the needs of the shepherds, ministries, missions, and activities of the church.

The following scripture verses outline the concept of grace giving.

- Luke 6:38 – Give, and it will be given to you: good measure, pressed down, shaken together, and running over will be put into your bosom. For with the same measure that you use, it will be measured back to you.
- This promise is for the person who has an attitude of grace and cheerfully gives out of the resources entrusted to him by God. The scope of this giving includes the person's time as well as his resources.
- Acts 20:35 – I have shown you in every way, by laboring like this, that you must support the weak. And remember the words of the Lord Jesus, that He said, "It is more blessed to give than to receive.
- II Corinthians 9:6 –But this I say: He who sows sparingly will also reap sparingly, and he who sows bountifully will also reap bountifully.
- This type of giving establishes the perimeters of grace giving. A person's dividends are in direct proportion to his investments. Every person has something to sow. Individuals are free to sow as the Lord directs knowing He will meet their needs(Proverbs 11:25).
- I Corinthians 3: 6-8 – I planted, Apollos watered, but God gave the increase. So then neither he who plants is anything, nor he who waters, but God who gives the increase. Now he who plants and

he who waters are one, and each one will receive his own reward according to his own labor.

- I Corinthians 9:7-14 – Who ever goes to war at his own expense? Who plants a vineyard and does not eat of its fruit? Or who tends a flock and does not drink of the milk of the flock? (8) Do I say these things as a mere man? Or does not the law say the same also? (9) For it is written in the law of Moses, "You shall not muzzle an ox while it treads out the grain." Is it oxen God is concerned about? (10) Or does He say it altogether for our sakes? For our sakes, no doubt, this is written, that he who plows should plow in hope, and he who threshes in hope should be partaker of his hope. (11) If we have sown spiritual things for you, is it a great thing if we reap your material things? (12) If others are partakers of this right over you, are we not even more? Nevertheless we have not used this right, but endure all things lest we hinder the gospel of Christ. (13) Do you not know that those who minister the holy things eat of the things of the temple, and those who serve at the altar partake of the offerings of the altar? (14) Even so the Lord has commanded that those who preach the gospel should live from the gospel.
- Galatians 6:6 –Let him who is taught the word share in all good things with him who teaches.
- Those that receive biblical teaching should support those who teach so they are free to prepare messages. (Acts 6:4).
- Romans 10:15 – And how shall they preach unless they are sent? As it is written: How beautiful are the feet of those who preach the gospel of peace. Who bring glad tidings of good things.
- Romans 15:27 – It pleased them indeed, and they are their debtors. For if the Gentiles have been partakers of their spiritual things, their duty is also to minister to them in material things.
- I Corinthians 9:11 – If we have sown spiritual things for you, is it a great thing if we reap your material things?
- There is a clear established biblical precedence that those who are sent by God to preach the gospel should be supported by the recipients of the good news he shares.
- These and other verses outline the Christian's responsibility for giving. The church leader should keep his congregation aware of

the necessary expenses needed for the ministries and maintenance of the church.

I Corinthians 9:7 – So let each one give as he purposes in his heart, not grudgingly or of necessity; for God loves a cheerful giver.

- Gracious giving originates in the heart not grudging or out of necessity.
- When we give as the Holy Spirit directs it brings joy to the soul (Proverbs 22:9).

- II Corinthians 9:8 – And God is able to make all grace abound toward you, that you, always having all sufficiency in all things, may have an abundance for every good work.
- This verse is the foundation for grace giving. God promises we will always have a sufficiency for our needs and an abundance to give to His ministries. This verse is not limited to just money. In the two previous verses He has outlined the attitude of grace givers. They sow bountifully out of a cheerful heart.
- II Corinthians 9:10 – Now may He who supplies seed to the sower, and bread for food, supply and multiply the seed you have sown and increase the fruits of your righteousness.
- Verse six and ten outline the principle of "sowing and reaping". God will provide everything we need in order to sow beyond our own needs. The promise is that if we sow as He directs, He will increase the fruits of our labor and count it as an act of righteousness.
- II Corinthians 9:12 – For the administration of this service not only supplies the needs of the saints, but also is abounding through many thanksgivings to God.
- Paul indicates that this type of sowing (giving) meets the needs of other Christians and results in much thanksgiving to God for His goodness.

II Corinthians 9:13 – While, through the proof of this ministry, they glorify God for the obedience of your confession to the gospel of Christ, and for your liberal sharing with them and all men

- Grace sharing is generous sharing.

- The motivation for grace giving is the realization that it is only by the grace of God that we are redeemed and blessed with all spiritual and physical blessings. Grace givers acknowledge that everything belongs to God and we are privileged to act as His representatives by giving as He directs. Grace is delighted to give as the Holy Spirit directs. Grace giving includes all manner of benevolent acts toward others. Grace does not give because it is required; it gives because it is a divine privilege. Grace givers do not feel guilty for not tithing; they enjoy an intimate relationship with God. The teaching of the principle of grace giving would free the pastor and church leader from having to pressure their congregation each Sunday for money.

The following are some additional thoughts and scriptures to ponder concerning tithing:

- None of the Old Testament tithers were born again. Christians through their new birth share a totally different relationship with Christ because they are in Christ and Christ is in them. A servant may be required to tithe but a son is not.

The spirit of Christians have become one with the Spirit of God. He has declared them to be joint heirs with Christ. Everything that they need for life and Godliness has been made available.

- 1 Peter 2:5 – you also, as living stones, are being built up a spiritual house, a holy priesthood, to offer up spiritual sacrifices acceptable to God through Jesus Christ.

  1 Peter 2:9 – But you are a chosen generation, a royal priesthood, a holy nation, His own special people, that you may proclaim the praises of Him who called you out of darkness into His marvelous light.
- Christians are holy priests and under the law priest were not required to tithe. Is the priesthood of the believer less than those of the Old Covenant?

My conclusion and conviction is there is no evidence the New Testament writings for Christians to tithe. All efforts to make it a requirement must be taken from Old Testament scriptures regarding a covenant that never applied to believers. The absence of any reference to tithing in the New Testament after the resurrection of Jesus should be ample evidence that tithing was not a requirement for the early church.

The New Testament shepherd must assume the responsibility for the spiritual wellbeing of his flock by rightly dividing the word of God. He should know the spiritual and physical condition of his sheep, and protect them from false doctrines and traditions. After His resurrection Jesus gave Peter specific instructions about how a shepherd should take care of his flock. The true shepherd will apply these guidelines to his own flock.

John 21:15-17 So when they had eaten breakfast, Jesus said to Simon Peter, "Simon, son of Jonah, do you love Me more than these? He said to Him, "Yes, Lord; You know that I love You." He said to him, "Feed my lambs." (16) He said to him again a second time, "Simon, son of Jonah, do you love Me? He said to Him, "Yes, Lord; You know that I love You." He said to him, "Tend My sheep." (17) He said to him the third time, "Simon, son of Johan, do you love Me?" Peter was grieved because He said to him the third time, "Do you love Me?' And he said to Him, "Lord, You know all things; You know that I love You." Jesus said to him, "Feed My sheep."

Jesus begins by directing Peter to "Feed my Lambs". Lambs represent new Christians or those who have very little knowledge of biblical truths. They are unable to understand and assimilate many of the scriptures. They are vulnerable to whatever is being taught from the pulpit. Therefore, the shepherd must recognize where they are at spiritually and feed them accordingly. The shepherd has the responsibility of guarding these lambs from the poison weeds of false doctrines.

Secondly, Jesus directs Peter to "Tend My sheep". Many who attend church have spiritual, physical, emotional, or various other types of problems that need special care. These problems consume their thinking to the point they are unable to concentrate on what is being shared from the pulpit. Unless they receive help for their problems the messages of truth intended for them goes unheeded. The good shepherd will know his flock well enough to realize their individual needs and will minister to those needs until the sheep find relief. Then they will be able to receive what he teaches. He will know their conditions by his personal visits and interests in their lives.

Finally, Jesus instructs Peter to, "Feed My sheep." The good shepherd recognizes those who are spiritually mature. He will provide them with spiritual food and guidance to equip them to pursue greater things for their church and God. These mature sheep will assume positions of responsibility in the church. The good shepherd is motivated in each of these areas because of his love for God and for his flock.

Printed in the United States
By Bookmasters

Printed in the United States
By Bookmasters